Managing Business Activities

Theme 2 for Edexcel Business AS and A Level

Alan Hewison

Brian Ellis

Alan Hewison is an experienced enthusiast for the courses which have evolved from the Nuffield Economics and Business project. He has taught, examined and written for these courses since their inception.

Brian Ellis has been involved in teaching, examining, curriculum development, teacher training and writing. He sees it as important for people to think and to smile sometimes.

© Anforme Ltd 2015
ISBN 978-1-78014-012-4
Images supplied by Shutterstock.com

Anforme Ltd, Stocksfield Hall, Stocksfield, Northumberland NE43 7TN.

Typeset by George Wishart & Associates, Whitley Bay.
Printed by Potts Print (UK) Ltd.

Contents

This book follows the specification sequence for theme 2 in the Edexcel AS and A level Business course from 2015. At the end of each of the five specification sections there is a question in the format to be expected in the Managing Business Activities exam paper. Three of these are data response questions and two are open-ended extended writing questions. Tackling these is intended to be part of the learning process as well as to introduce students to the types of questions they will meet.

We are very grateful to the businesses which have allowed us to use their experience to give real contexts for business ideas. In the case of small businesses, we have changed names when asked to and have simplified some situations. However, we have tried to stay real rather than rely on fictional case studies.

We are also grateful to everyone, too many people to name, whose ideas have contributed to the earlier books (and courses) on which this is built.

The mistakes herein are ours.

Chapter 1

Raising finance: internal

Tangle Teezers

Shaun Pulfrey describes his former self as "the go-to guy in hairdressing salons for getting tangles out of hair." His ideas for a better brush to tackle tangles became the foundation for Tangle Teezers. In his view the most difficult thing about starting the business was sacrificing his normal life. He did not go out. All his energy and money was poured into making it work. It was quite solitary too, spending hours in the British Library reading up on injection plastic moulding and patents. "From a guy that loved to socialise, I went to a person who didn't go on holidays, buy clothes or see friends properly for about three years."

Financing the business was another problem. He made a pitch on Dragons' Den but was turned down. Despite this, viewers who saw the show sent in about 1,500 orders. He re-mortgaged his flat in London to keep going for 6 months. The business took off, with rapid expansion and a Queen's Award for Enterprise in Innovation. The brushes are now widely available and the firm's value was estimated in 2015 at £65m.

Questions

1. How did Shaun's appearance on Dragons' Den affect his business?
2. What could Shaun have done if the business failed?

The financial crisis that began in 2008 made finance much harder to obtain as banks and other organisations restricted their lending. Since then the situation has improved a little, but the CBI (Confederation of British Industry) reports that although traditional forms of finance, such as overdrafts and loans, are still the main source of finance (UK banks account for nearly 80% of all credit) businesses are increasingly looking to alternative finance options. Some of these such as crowdfunding and peer-to-peer funding are examined in the next section.

Businesses now have an increasing choice of lenders, with new so-called 'challenger banks' entering the market. Two of them, Shawbrook and Aldermore, increased their loans and advances to customers by 82.8% and 52.7% respectively between 2012 and 2014. There has also been an increase in the use of equity financing (finance that is given in exchange for a share in the business) such as business angels, some types of crowdfunding and venture capital, but there is still a long way to go compared to other countries. Just 3% of SMEs (small and medium-sized businesses) use equity finance in the UK, while the EU average is 7% and in countries such as Denmark and Sweden, it accounts for 46% and 31% of SME financing respectively.

> **Finance** is the money that businesses need to start and to operate. Businesses need finance at different times and for a number of different reasons.

Start-ups

Starting a new business involves numerous costs. Some of these will be large one-off payments for things like premises and equipment and can be extensive. In its early days the business may also need finance to pay costs such as wages and raw materials until it becomes established and generates enough income from its sales. Finding start-up funding is often a major challenge to new businesses. Underestimating how much is needed is a route to rapid disaster.

Working capital

If all goes well, a business will eventually begin to make a profit. However, profit is not the same as cash (working capital) and cash is the lifeblood of a business. Sometimes a business will have to pay bills before receiving revenue from its sales. Without sufficient cash the business will not be able to pay its bills on a day-to-day basis and may get into trouble. This means that additional finance is needed on a temporary basis to provide sufficient working capital to cope with any cash flow problems.

> ### Activity
> Imagine you are thinking of starting a business and setting up a mobile sandwich, snack and cake delivery service for office workers in a nearby business park.
>
> List as many reasons as you can think of for this business needing finance, both now and in the future.
>
> Where would you get it from?

Depreciation – depreciation is a term that describes the loss in value of assets (things of value). For example a new delivery van may cost £25,000 but a year later is only worth £20,000. Three years later it is only worth £10,000 and may need replacing. It has depreciated by £15,000. When the business needs to buy a new one, finance will be needed. This principle applies to many other physical assets, machinery wears out and needs replacing, buildings need repairing, and computer systems need upgrading. All of this is likely to require the use of finance.

Expansion – There may come a time when the business will want to expand. This may be in the form of physical expansion such as new buildings, extra productive capacity or extending the scope of its sales by launching into new markets with extra promotion and distribution costs. All this is likely to involve the need for extra finance to pay for it.

Finance is available from a number of sources. Each source has its advantages and disadvantages for the business and each will be appropriate in different situations. Access to a particular kind of finance may also be determined by the type and size of a business. Businesses must decide between a range of Internal and External sources of finance. Businesses, particularly larger ones, may use a number of sources both internal and external.

Internal finance

> These terms mean what they say… if the finance comes from *inside* the business it is **Internal**. If the finance comes from *outside* the business it is **External**.

Figure 1.1: Internal sources of finance

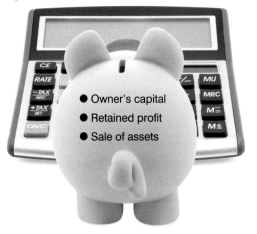

- Owner's capital
- Retained profit
- Sale of assets

The great advantage of internal finance is that it should cost less than external finance because interest payments will be lower or non-existent. When owners put in their own finance, they are losing only the interest that the money might have made in a savings account. (This is the opportunity cost of the funds.) Similarly, retained profits are the savings of the company. They have an opportunity cost but the interest lost will be less than the interest that would have to be paid on a loan from the bank. Selling assets that are not being utilised frees up cash for other purposes. There may be selling costs, but there will be no interest to pay.

Owner's capital: personal savings

Owner's capital refers to any monies that the owner may have access to. It is sometimes referred to as Owner's equity. This may be in the form of savings built up over time; it may come from an inheritance or from a redundancy payment. It is estimated that more than one in six new business start-ups are established following redundancy. Using your own capital has the advantage that it does not have to be repaid and carries no interest charges. It may also help in obtaining further finance once the business is established, as other lenders may be more willing to lend if the owner has a personal stake in the business.

Use of savings is best suited for sole trader and partnership start-ups, but the very real risk of the business not succeeding means that the owner's capital can be lost. Before sinking savings into a business, it is important to weigh up the risk of losing these savings realistically. Risk averse people will think carefully first, but many new entrepreneurs are unrealistically optimistic. New internet based businesses can often require less start-up finance than other types of business – with no dedicated business premises, for example. Such businesses have the advantage that less is being risked.

New partnerships often involve an entrepreneur who will take charge of business working together with a partner who takes little or no part in day to day decision making but contributes most or all of the starting capital. This requires strong trust between the partners and clear decisions on how any profits will be shared.

Retained profit

Retained profit is all the money that is left after all deductions have been taken away from total sales revenue including tax, interest and any dividends paid to shareholders. It can then potentially be re-invested into the business. It is usually regarded as one of the best forms of finance to use as it belongs to the business already and does not involve debt. There is no need to pay it back and there is no interest to pay for its use. An economist would argue that there is an opportunity cost. For the business owner(s) this could mean not taking any dividend or other form of profit, so that the maximum possible retained profit is available to finance expansion.

For many businesses the main disadvantage here is that the level of retained profits may not be large enough to meet their finance needs. Waiting for more retained profit to accumulate can mean losing potentially profitable business opportunities. It is also unsuitable for start-ups as by their very nature they will not have any retained profits.

Sale of assets

All businesses have assets (things of value e.g. buildings, land, vehicles, machinery) and these can be sold in order to raise money. In some circumstances this can be very beneficial. It may be that a business has some land or buildings that it no longer requires, perhaps because it now outsources some or all of its production. Alternatively, a business might have developed several products before deciding to focus on one profitable area. Surplus assets can be sold to raise finance that does not need to be repaid or carry interest charges.

Sometimes a business will sell assets such as vehicles or machinery and then lease or rent the assets back again, trading off the financial gain against continuous future payments. This assumes that a business has assets to sell in the first place; many businesses will be making full use of their assets and be unable to operate without them. A business 'sitting on' valuable but unused assets will appear not to be using current finance very efficiently. Once again, this method of finance is unsuitable for start-ups as they will not have any assets yet.

Chapter 2

External finance

Cheese Posties

Kickstarter is a crowdfunding platform. This means that would-be entrepreneurs can use the site to invite anyone interested in helping to finance a business venture.

Dave Rotheroe thinks there could be a market for 'Cheese Posties'. His plan is to mail out a different grilled cheese sandwich to subscribers each week. High quality ingredients, such as artisan bread and fine cheeses, will offer 'Mouth-watering melting combos'. Examples mentioned on Kickstarter include 'balsamic blueberry and cream cheese' and 'chocolate cheesecake'.

People who gave funding were promised rewards tied to the amount pledged. £5 or £10 pledges were mainly rewarded with Cheese Posties. By late June 2015, around 150 backers had promised the £2,000 Dave wanted. They were only charged when the target was reached.

Questions

1. In your opinion, are Cheese Posties a viable business?
2. Could Dave have financed Cheese Posties with his own money?
3. Apart from not using any savings he had, what other advantages does using Kickstarter offer?

External finance requires some other person(s) or organisation to give up the use of their money so that you can spend it. Most often, they will need either interest payments or part-ownership to persuade them to do this, though there are exceptions (such as Cheese Posties). There are more external sources than internal ones, and most businesses will have to rely on them at one time or another.

Figure 2.1: External sources of finance

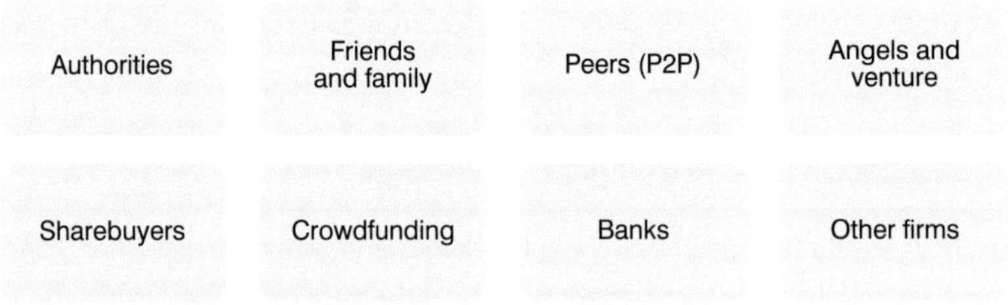

Authorities	Friends and family	Peers (P2P)	Angels and venture
Sharebuyers	Crowdfunding	Banks	Other firms

Authorities and donors

The government and local authorities provide a wide range of financial and other support for businesses in the form of grants, subsidies and tax relief schemes (the gov.uk website currently lists 603 such schemes!). The enterprise allowance helps those who qualify with living costs when they start a business. Other organisations support things such as environmentally friendly start-ups. The Prince's Trust particularly helps young entrepreneurs.

Family and friends

Older relatives might have retirement or other savings which earn little interest, combined with a desire to support members of their family. Friends might share enthusiasm for a business idea and be willing to offer some finance if they are able to. There are advantages to finance from family or friends rather than other sources. They are more likely to be flexible and relaxed about terms and conditions, and may offer loans without security or accept less security than banks. They may also provide interest-free or low rate finance and be happy with a longer repayment period. Parents or grandparents might even give money. One way to formalise arrangements with family and friends is to form a private limited company (see share issues below).

Banks

Banks are financial intermediaries. Their business is to hold savings for those who have them and to lend out money to borrowers. The best known are the big 4 high street banks, who offer services to both new and established businesses and usually a quick decision process. Although different high street banks offer similar services, a business customer would be well advised to shop around for the best deal. Banks will want some form of security if they are to loan money to a business.

Other banks are also available. Challenger banks are expanding rapidly. Private Banks such as Coutts offer lending services. There are specialised social finance banks and other financial bodies that can provide finance for social enterprises and co-operatives. The Islamic Bank of Britain and many other banks provide Sharia-compliant lending which is acceptable to Muslims.

Peers (P2P)

The first building societies were clubs where people jointly contributed savings and used loans for house purchase (in turn) when funds were available. Initially, members came from the same community. Nowadays, websites can bring lenders and borrowers together. They can cut out the banking intermediaries and so offer savers a better return and borrowers lower interest charges.

Zopa is currently the UK's largest peer-to-peer lending service and expects to have lent over £1bn by the end of 2015. Zopa will lend up to £25,000 to sole traders who have been operating for at least two years. It is therefore not suitable for larger businesses or start-ups.

Angels and Venture Capital

Business Angels are usually high-net worth individuals who invest in early stage or high growth businesses, either directly or through organised networks such as the Enterprise Investment Scheme or Seed Enterprise Investment Scheme. These government backed schemes are designed to help smaller early-stage businesses and/or higher-risk businesses raise finance by offering a range of tax reliefs to investors who invest in these companies.

The CBI estimates that there are approximately 18,000 business angels in the UK, investing an estimated £850m per annum. They are normally knowledgeable and experienced in business and can act as a mentor for the business, providing useful advice and guidance for a growing business. Business angels are particularly well suited to businesses looking for early funding to grow rapidly.

Business Angels are also called Venture Capitalists. Some of them use their own money but there are also Venture Capital Funds where money put into the fund (by many people) is spread across a variety of growing businesses (chosen by specialist managers) to spread risk.

Sharebuyers

Shares represent part ownership (a share) in a business. As part owners, shareholders are entitled to part of the profits and to a say in running the business. This is one way of setting up an arrangement with family and friends, using the private limited company (Ltd) system. Private Companies are generally smaller firms.

Public companies (PLCs) follow more complex rules (such as issuing a prospectus giving details on the business) and can issue (sell) shares to the public. This is rarely an option for new businesses, but it can fund expansion once a firm is established. For example, Sophos is a cyber-security business; its customers include the BBC and the NHS. It is expecting to raise £100m by going public and to be valued at about £1bn. It will use the finance to reduce its debt and consolidate its position as one of the leaders in its field.

Crowdfunding

New and small businesses conventionally raise finance from one or a few sources. Crowdfunding does the opposite and raises finance by asking large numbers of people for a small sum of money. The Statue of Liberty was financed this way long ago, but the internet, whereby millions of potential funders can be reached, has taken crowdfunding to a new level. Those seeking finance can post a profile of their business venture on numerous websites and appeal for investors. They can use other forms of social media to publicise their projects.

There are different types of crowdfunding:

Donation/Reward crowdfunding – Investors donate money because they believe in the ideas of the business. Such ventures may well be artistic or altruistic; the return for investors is a reward of some kind, a free t-shirt, free gifts, tickets to an event, Cheese Posties and so on.

Equity crowdfunding – People invest in an opportunity in exchange for a share in the business. Money is exchanged for shares, or a small stake in the business, project or venture. The process is similar to a traditional share issue.

Activity

www.buzzbnk.org   www.crowdfunder.co.uk   www.angelsden.com

Visit these websites and have a look at how they operate, note the wide range of different ventures and finance requirements. Look at how businesses can gain finance and the conditions under which it is given.

Choose two projects you would invest in and two you would not – explain your reasons.

Other businesses

Businesses which see a firm as a customer (e.g. for services or raw materials) or a supplier if they use or retail the product, have an interest in the firm's success. Most often they will help in ways tied to deals between the two businesses. Occasionally a bigger established firm will take a smaller one 'under its wing' and offer support and finance either with a loan or for a share of ownership.

The most frequent way of supporting client firms is **trade credit**. Suppliers allow 30 days (sometimes more) after delivering supplies before payment is due. This allows retailers, for example, to sell some stock before they pay for it. **Factoring** means selling an invoice for goods a firm has supplied on credit before payment is due. The buyer gets a discounted price in return for holding the invoice until payment is made. **Leasing** and **hire purchase** are ways of renting assets rather than buying them. This saves the expense of paying 'up front'. The difference between the two is that hire purchase agreements end with the asset owned by the firm using it; leased assets go back to the owner and the user often takes a new lease on fresh assets.

Figure 2.2: Methods of external finance

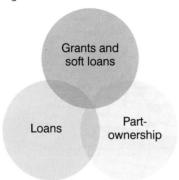

Grants and soft loans

> **Soft loans** are funds made available at favourable terms for the borrower, less than normal commercial interest rates.

People generally offer grants and soft loans either because they want to support the borrower (friends and family) or because they support what the business is doing. For example, government provides start-up grants and loans in areas with high unemployment such as the North East and Cumbria. To be eligible for this scheme you must be aged 18 or over and living in the area, and your business must be under 12 months old or in the planning stage. If successful a grant of up to £25,000 is possible. Other schemes aim to support exporters.

There really are a lot of schemes out there, try looking at https://www.gov.uk/browse/business/finance-support to see what is available and who is eligible.

Free (grants) or cheap money is obviously attractive and friends and family can offer good support for small firms. However, there are potential drawbacks to this sort of funding; a misunderstanding can damage relationships. There is the obvious risk that the business may fail and they lose their money. They may offer more than they can really afford to lose, or they may demand their money back when it suits them but not the business. They may also want to get more involved in the business, which the entrepreneur might not want. Government and charitable organisations often bundle useful advice with grants or soft loans. However, they are likely to want checks that the firm will do what they want done. This can involve copious form filling and continuing checks that can become a chore.

Loans

The big advantage of a loan is that the borrower keeps ownership and control of the firm and once it is repaid there is no further payment or loss of profit. The interest payable is usually fixed, so if the firm does well it will be manageable. Lenders want security that they will get their money back, preferably with interest. This can involve **collateral**, such as a claim on your house, and many lenders want to look into how safe the business is as a borrower and how much the entrepreneur has put in from their own assets. This often entails preparing a detailed **business plan** (see Chapter 4).

> Property or other assets that a borrower offers a lender to secure a loan becomes **collateral**. If the borrower stops making the promised payments, the lender can claim the collateral to recover the debt.

Peer-to-peer lending has expanded rapidly.

Loans can be expensive, though P2P loans are generally cheaper than banks. Failure to repay a loan can mean the end of a business. A lender becomes a creditor and can take action to force the closure of a firm and sale of its assets in order to get back what they can. Any collateral can also be claimed to repay the debt. Whereas banks will normally give quick decisions, P2P loan requests can sit on websites for a period of time with no certainty that enough lenders will sign up. The after-effects of the financial crisis of 2008 made obtaining credit from banks much harder, particularly for small businesses and start-ups.

Banks, the main traditional lenders, offer two types of lending. A bank loan (like many other loans) has an agreed schedule of repayments at set times. A repayment loan is most often linked to new equipment or small-scale expansion, something repayable within two or so years. An overdraft is an agreement that allows a firm to borrow what it needs up to a set limit, with interest charged on what is actually used. So, for example, a house builder using an overdraft for working capital might increase the overdraft as costs mount up through a project, but then reduce or end the overdraft when the houses are sold. One downside of an overdraft is that the agreement is subject to periodic renewal. In the last recession banks effectively forced many firms out of business by not renewing overdrafts.

Part-ownership (shares)

There are several means of funding which entail shares or similar part-ownership being exchanged for the injection of funds. The advantage these all share is that the money need never be repaid by the business. Shareholders who want money back have to find someone to sell their shares to. There isn't even any interest to be paid. An extra advantage with Business Angels/Venture Capitalists is that they tend to have experience of business strategy and can often give wise advice together with the funding.

There are two big drawbacks. The first of these is that new part-owners become entitled to share in profits and to have a say in how the business is run. The previous owner(s) retain some shares but can become a minority. With a PLC, for example, owners of 51% of share capital can instruct the directors on what to do. If a 'hostile' larger firm acquires 51% of the shares, they can force through a takeover and replace the original directors.

Shareholders' profit payments, called dividends, are in proportion to the share of the business owned. Paying dividends leaves less for the original owners, so a loan could be cheaper for a very profitable firm.

Sometimes a dividend may still be paid even if the company makes a loss, in order to keep shareholders happy and prevent them from selling shares – which would cause the value of the company to drop. Adidas ended 2014 reporting a net loss of €139 million in the final quarter but still paid a dividend.

The formalities and expense of a public share issue make this unsuitable for a small firm. Crowdfunding or venture capital might be more suitable. Crowdfunding success is even less predictable than P2P loans. Against that, even an untried new business idea can sometimes get crowdfunding.

Venture capitalists invest in early stage, high-risk businesses with the potential for high returns or potential for high-growth. They are hard-nosed and experienced at negotiating bargains which give them a big slice of future profits. Against that, their specialist skills can help a small business move up to bigger things. Quite often, these investors will want to move on after 5 years or so, selling their stake in the business back to the founder(s) or on to new investors.

Methods of finance summary

Type	Best suited to	Main Advantages	Main Disadvantages
Internal	Rich people and firms with profits from past.	No cash cost/terms. Helps security for added external finance.	Opportunity cost. Carry all the risk.
Grants and soft loans	Start-up, small and innovating firms. Exporters.	Free or cheap. Simple (family/friends).	Complex process and conditions/expectations (especially government).
Loans	Short/medium term. Firms with collateral.	Limited duration. Often cheaper if P2P.	Fees and interest possibly high. Must be repaid or closure of firm likely.
Part-ownership	Small Ltd company. Expanding firm. Crowdfunding possibly for Start-ups.	No set repayment. Angels/venture can bring good advice.	Future profits shared. Might lose some control to newcomers. PLC set-up expensive.

Chapter 3

Liability

Lloyds of London

Lloyds of London (not the bank) is a global insurance market, with historical roots in a coffee house. It is possible to take out insurance policies at Lloyds on almost anything. Dancer Michael Flatley took out a £multi-million policy against losing the use of his legs, Costa took a policy against their chief coffee taster losing his sense of taste. 'Underwriters' decide the premium (charge) to offer on policies. 'Names' of well-off people, in groups or 'syndicates', are paid to take the risk – then they must pay up if a successful claim is made on a policy.

Late in the last century there was a major scandal, when massive court judgements for workers suffering the effects of asbestos had to be paid by the insurers. Many people who became 'names' lost everything. They had unlimited liability which meant that all their possessions could be taken to pay the bills. The scandal centred on suspicion that some names were promised easy money to get them to sign up, by people who knew that massive claims were on the way.

Questions

1. Why would people want to risk everything, as 'names' did?
2. How much safer than Lloyds names is a small shopkeeper with unlimited liability?

Unlimited liability

Liability in business is about risk taking and financial responsibility. Many people are reluctant to take risks (risk averse) and so are put off business by the risks involved. Some businesses not only lose their owners any money they have put into the business if it fails, the owners are also responsible for any debts the business has. These are businesses with **unlimited liability**.

Business owners that operate with unlimited liability have to personally repay any debts incurred by their business to the full extent of their means and their assets. A creditor can pursue a sole trader or partnership through the courts to get their money back. Everything the debtor possesses, such as savings, investments, furniture, car and home, may have to be sold to pay the debts. This may end up in the debtor becoming bankrupt. (Note that 'bankruptcy' only applies to individuals.)

For a sole trader, this means that the owner has to take responsibility for any debts the business incurs. At least this is most often the result of that person's decisions. In most partnerships each partner has unlimited liability, so one partner could lose their property to pay for another partner's mistakes. This makes people who are risk averse very cautious about going into a partnership with anyone they don't know well and trust thoroughly.

In theory other businesses should be more willing to trade with, and offer credit terms to, businesses with unlimited liability because they have a good chance of getting their money back if things go wrong.

> A **creditor** is a person or a business to which money is owed, either for providing supplies or finance. A **debtor** is a person or business that owes money to a creditor.
>
> **Bankruptcy** is an official (court) finding that a person has more liabilities than assets so is unable to pay all of their debts.

Limited liability

Buying shares to become part-owner of a company would be very risky if it involved unlimited liability. The main reason why companies have **limited liability** is to increase people's willingness to buy shares by reducing the risks involved. Many countries divide companies into two types. In the UK we have private companies, required by law to include 'Ltd' at the end of their name and public companies which are each a 'Plc'. In Germany, the letters GmbH are used for their private company equivalent and AG for a public company. In the USA it is LLC and Inc. respectively.

> Over half a million new companies are registered in the UK each year. A widely accepted estimate is that half of new companies go into liquidation within 5 years. The failure rate is higher in some activities. Around 80% of small clothing retail outlets close within 5 years of opening, and around 60% of independent restaurants. UK government data suggests that only 30% of companies are still trading 10 years after they are first registered.

The same rules which protect shareholders transfer risk, in effect, to creditors. These are people who are owed money by a business. Should a business fail before paying them, they will only get their money back if the business itself has enough assets and they have no claim against shareholders.

When a company becomes insolvent, which means when the company cannot pay its debts, it ceases to trade and is liquidated, in other words its assets are sold to raise cash which is used to pay at least some of its debts. Some companies become insolvent when owing enormous sums which they cannot repay. The owners are protected by law; their personal possessions cannot be used to repay the company's debts.

There is a much greater risk for those dealing with limited companies that become insolvent, compared to businesses with unlimited liability. The owners have transferred much, if not most of the risk to suppliers, customers and employees. Suppliers may not get paid, customers can lose their deposits, customers can be left with worthless guarantees, employees may not be paid for work done and other monies owed by the enterprise may not be repaid. Suppliers and customers lose large sums each year. The law gives priority to some creditors. Tax authorities and workers have higher priority than suppliers or customers, for example.

> **Liability** means responsibility for the financial debts of the business.
>
> **Sole traders** and **partnerships** have **unlimited liability** which means that the owners have a legal responsibility for all debts and can have all of their personal possessions seized to pay them.
>
> **Limited companies** exist legally as separate from their owners. The company may fail and lose its assets, but the personal wealth of the owners is separate in law so not at risk.

Summary table

	Business types	Risk in trading with them
Unlimited liability	Sole traders and partnerships	Lower as owners assets can be claimed
Limited liability	Companies: Ltd & Plc	Higher, only business assets are at risk

Find out

Try a Google search (or newspaper archive) for recent liquidations.

Pick one and work out which groups of people are likely to have lost money as a result.

Limitations to the real differences

Sole traders and partners have unlimited liability. They will not want their families to suffer if the business fails. If their homes, for example, are owned by their wives, or even jointly owned, it is hard for creditors to take them. Using this fact, some business owners transfer valuable assets to relatives or to trusts, so minimising the amount they risk and creditors could take. This is essentially legal. Others act illegally, trying to hide their assets and lie about what they are worth. Either way, such actions reduce the security that unlimited liability can give creditors.

Many owners of private companies make their businesses Ltd in order to have limited liability, (though there are also some tax advantages as another incentive). Because banks and major lenders understand limited liability, they often insist on director's guarantees before parting with any money. Any company director that signs a director guarantee is giving a personal guarantee that she/he will be liable for the company's debt or commitment if the company is liquidated and does not settle its debt. This means that personal assets can be seized in the event of a limited company becoming insolvent in much the same way as a sole trader's. Ideally, lenders like collateral, which uses specific assets to guarantee repayment.

This risk in dealing with limited companies is why the larger public companies also have to file annual independently audited accounts, as well as information about the directors with Companies House. This information is available to all who wish to check a company's creditworthiness, performance and progress. However, it takes time and money to obtain the information and knowledge and experience to understand, interpret and analyse the published data.

Some industries have made arrangements to compensate customers losing out from liquidations. Their trade associations have created funds by collecting contributions from member companies. In the event of one of their member companies becoming insolvent compensation is paid to customers who lose out. This reassures customers so they are more willing to buy. Unfortunately, many of the riskier companies don't join such schemes or are in industries where they don't exist.

ABTA the Travel Association (previously called the Association of British Travel Agents) is designed to protect all customers who buy a land- or sea-based holiday such as a coach, rail or cruise holiday from an ABTA member. This means that if your travel company fails and your holiday can no longer

Private company shareholders benefit from limited liability.

go ahead you will be entitled to a refund if you are yet to travel, or hotel costs and transport home if you are abroad.

ATOL stands for Air Travel Organisers' Licence. It is a government-run financial protection scheme operated by the Civil Aviation Authority (CAA). ATOL cover means that if your travel company fails and your holiday can no longer go ahead you will be entitled to a refund if you are yet to travel and hotel costs and flights home if you are abroad.

A minority of limited companies do exploit their limited liability status unfairly. A company may be registered, start trading, become insolvent and cease to trade after having incurred considerable debts which it cannot repay. The owners and directors of that insolvent company may then register another company under a new name and continue trading under the new name, with similar results and more losses to the public. Television programmes such as Watchdog frequently highlight such cases.

Many companies are responsible and reliable; dealings with them are relatively safe. However, new and unscrupulous companies are riskier and can exploit limited liability to their own advantage. This helps to explain why dealing with companies is seen as riskier.

Finance appropriate for limited and unlimited liability businesses

In principle, unlimited liability should make businesses a safer debtor if you have dealings with them. This should make it easier for them to borrow loans, as lenders have more security. However, sensible lenders often seek the reassurance that these businesses have plenty of assets from owners' capital or/and retained profits to reduce the chance of them losing their money.

Sole traders and partnerships do not have the right to issue shares, so they cannot raise money in that way. Private limited companies can only sell shares to friends and family, they cannot advertise shares to the public. This limits their access to share capital unless the people involved are very wealthy.

Going public, as a Plc, is the route to large scale share issues. This is why a few large scale new businesses (such as Eurotunnel when it started) are set up as Plcs. More often, existing businesses 'go public' by becoming Plcs when they want finance for large scale expansion. Their size, and often also their assets, help Plcs to overcome the relative insecurity of limited liability and obtain loans. Overdrafts and short to medium term bank loans are actually held by many businesses of all types.

Finance availability summary chart

Type of finance	Sole trader and partnership	Private company Ltd	Public company Plc
Owners capital	Yes	Yes, as shares	Yes, as shares
Grants/soft loans	Yes, if possible	Yes, if possible	Yes, if possible
Retained profits	Yes, if they exist	Yes, if they exist	Yes, if they exist
Share issues	No	Restricted	Yes
Loans	Yes, if felt safe	Yes, if felt safe	Yes, if felt safe

Chapter 4

Planning

The Traveller's rest

Lucie and Nathan worked for years as pub managers. When the lease for The Traveller's Rest pub/restaurant in Trevarrian (Cornwall) became available, they had around half of the funding required, but needed help. A High Street bank decided that a loan to them would be secure, helped by a detailed business plan, including a cash flow forecast.

The couple won their brewery's 2013 new tenant award and their business is thriving. Most reviewers rate The Traveller's Rest as excellent.

Questions

1. Why might the bank have been pleased that Lucie and Nathan also used their own savings?

2. Why is a business plan important to lenders?

3. How reliable is the cash forecast in a business plan?

A business plan is something that all businesses, particularly new and start-up businesses, should have. Its role in helping to obtain finance is explained below, but it is also a valuable management tool. It helps the owner to think in detail about the business and where it is going in the future and to set realistic targets, it also becomes a useful yardstick by which to measure progress.

> A **business plan** is a document that sets out what the business is, what it does and what it wants to achieve and how it is going to do it. It is normally used as part of an attempt to gain financial backing for the business.

Relevance of a business plan in obtaining finance

Preparing a good business plan is important in obtaining finance. It helps potential lenders or investors both to understand what the business is trying to achieve and to assess whether to provide finance or not. It brings focus to the business strategy and helps in assessing the impact of any changes from the plan, particularly when it comes to funding. Raising finance is difficult enough in today's economic environment and a well-produced business plan can make a big difference.

When seeking investment via a plan, it is important to describe clearly the opportunity, investors will want to know why they should provide finance for that particular business, rather than another. The actual content of the plan may vary depending on the nature of the business and its purpose but there are a number of items that should be in it.

● Executive Summary – this is a brief overview of the whole plan, designed to give potential backers a quick idea of what the business is about and to persuade them to read on.

● The business and its products/services – this part of the plan sets the vision for the business and includes what it is and what it does. It should include information about the nature of the product or service, what will make it special and what its competitive advantage may be.

● The market and competitors – this section should describe the target market and also look at the competition and how the market may change. It should be based on accurate market research.

- The marketing plan – this section should describe the specific activities to promote and sell the products or services. It will also include details of the pricing strategy.

- Organisational details – provides detail on the human resources involved, covering the background and skills of managers and staff. It should identify any strengths and plans to deal with any weaknesses.

- The production plan – shows how the business plans to produce and deliver the products or services, with details about premises and equipment needed. It will also explain what inputs are needed and detail the suppliers and other necessary business relationships.

- Historic financial records – covering the last few years of trading (if available) – accounts (audited if available), and key accounting ratios. This section will not be present for new businesses and start-ups.

- Financial forecasts – a very important section. The plan should have a set of financial projections which show how the business hopes to progress over time. These should include a cash flow forecast, break-even analysis and an income statement. It will be important to explain assumptions made about prices, costs and sales revenue.

- Existing sources of finance – anyone who is being asked to help finance the business will want to know what existing sources of finance the business already has. Banks seldom lend to entrepreneurs who are not prepared to put their own savings into the business.

A well-written business plan can help convey vital points to prospective investors, helping them to feel confident in the business and in the thoroughness with which it has considered future scenarios. The most crucial component will be clear evidence of the company's future ability to generate sufficient cash flows to meet debt obligations and enable the business to operate effectively. If a bank is made more confident, for example, the firm might even be offered a lower rate of interest.

> ### Activity
> If you were thinking of investing in a business what would you need to know before deciding?
>
> Make a list of as many points as possible, explaining why they are important.

Interpretation of a simple cash-flow forecast

A cash flow forecast is an attempt to look at the flows of cash in and out of a business over a period of time. It helps to predict times when there may be a shortage of cash and therefore a need to borrow (often an overdraft). It takes the form of a spreadsheet showing month by month what is happening to cash entering and leaving the business.

> A **cash flow forecast** is a month by month prediction of the timings of expected cash inflows, outflows and balances for a business.

Cash inflows are the monies gained from sales, finance and any other income the business has. Cash outflows are payments made for all the costs of a business such as materials, labour, rent, capital costs and loan repayments.

If more money is coming into the business than going out, there is a **positive** cash flow. If more money is going out of the business than coming in there is a **negative** cash flow. This needs addressing to avoid running out of working capital and being unable to pay the bills.

A simple cash flow forecast – figures in brackets mean a minus figure:

	January £	February £	March £	April £	May £	June £
Cash inflow						
Opening balance	0	1,000	1,500	2,000	(2,500)	(1,000)
Sales revenue	5,000	11,000	13,000	14,000	16,000	17,000
Loans	10,000					
Total cash inflow	**15,000**	**11,000**	**13,000**	**14,000**	**16,000**	**17,000**
Cash outflow						
Stock	8,000	8,000	10,000	12,000	12,000	12,000
Wages	2,000	2,000	2,000	2,000	2,000	2,000
Advertising	1,000			1,000		
Loan repayment	0	500	500	500	500	500
Rent	3,000			3,000		
Total cash outflow	**14,000**	**10,500**	**12,500**	**18,500**	**14,500**	**14,500**
Net cash flow	**1,000**	**500**	**500**	**(4,500)**	**1,500**	**2,500**
Closing balance	1,000	1,500	2,000	(2,500)	(1,000)	1,500

Interpretation:

Opening balance = what is in the bank on the first day of the month

Total cash inflow = all monies entering the business in that month

Total cash outflow = all monies leaving the business in that month

Net cash flow = Total cash inflow – Total cash outflow

Closing balance = Opening balance + Net cash flow

The story behind the numbers

In **January** a new business starts up with a loan of £10,000; sales are low at £5,000 so the total cash inflow for January is £15,000. Costs need to be paid including paying for stock and wages, the first 3 months' rent in advance and some advertising, so there is a total cash outflow of £14,000. The net cash flow is £1,000 (£15,000 – £14,000). This forms both the closing balance and also the opening balance for the next month.

In **February** and **March** sales increase, as do some of the costs, and the closing balance increases to £2,000.

In **April**, the next quarter's rent falls due and some more advertising is bought. This creates a negative cash flow and the balance is a (minus) figure i.e. the business cannot finance its cash flow. The closing balance is now (£2,500). This tells the business that it must make arrangements to fund this negative balance.

Things improve in **May** and the net cash flow returns to positive, *but* there is still a negative closing balance, so once again the business will need to seek extra finance.

In **June** the business returns to a positive closing balance.

Having produced this forecast the business can see the problem that will arise in April and May and plan for it, perhaps by arranging an overdraft with the bank. The bank will want to see this forecast and see that in June, the business is once again expecting a positive cash flow.

Exam tip

You will **not** be asked to construct a cash flow forecast from scratch, but you could be asked to add to one or to comment on the implications of a forecast for a business.

Use and limitations of a cash-flow forecast

Cash to a business is the equivalent of oil to an engine; without it the business or engine will seize up and grind to a halt. Cash needs to be constantly circulating around the business, which is why it is referred to as a flow. Careful management of cash flow is a fundamental requirement for all businesses.

Any forecast uses estimates, and life rarely works out exactly as we expect and estimate in advance. A cash flow forecast is a valuable working document that needs checking and updating, it is not just there to raise finance in a business plan and then forget. The reason that many businesses fail is not because they are unprofitable, but because they run out of cash (working capital). They cannot pay their debts when they are due.

Think!

Did all of yesterday work out exactly as you would have predicted?

Cash flow management becomes even more vital when businesses pursue investment opportunities involving significant cash outflows before any new cash flows come in. A well-structured forecast will help manage funding requirements in advance.

A cash flow forecast has other uses besides warning of future problems that require extra finance. They can be a useful way of looking at 'what if…' scenarios. What happens to cash flow if sales fall by 10%? What happens to cash outflow if higher wages are paid? By changing figures in the cash flow forecast, different scenarios can be played out and plans made in advance to cope with the results.

As time passes actual figures can be compared to the forecast's figures. This may show where problems have occurred and suggest where improvements in managing the finances of the business can be made.

It may sound strange, but too much cash can also be a problem for a business, as cash is far more useful when it is invested in expanding the business rather than just sitting in a bank account. The ideal is to keep the level of working capital just right, not too little and not too much. A cash flow forecast can show when there is too much cash as well as too little.

Cash flow forecasts are just that – forecasts. They are a bit are like weather forecasts, they can be inaccurate and the further ahead you try and predict, the greater the error is likely to be. There is no guarantee that even the most carefully thought out financial projections will turn out to be realistic. They are predictions; sales may not be as high as expected, costs may change, business rivals may react and affect your planning, the economy might go into a downturn, the government may increase taxes and so on.

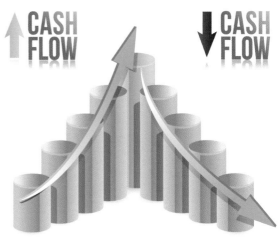

If a cash flow forecast is checked and updated regularly it is a useful guide, besides being essential to a business plan and any application for finance.

Activity

The figures for January and February have been entered. Rent is paid every three months and advertising every alternate month.

Fill in the blanks for the rest of the table. Remember that 'minus' or negative figures are put into brackets.

In which month will the business need extra finance?

Would you recommend the business to take out a loan or an overdraft? Justify your choice.

	January £	February £	March £	April £	May £	June £
Cash inflow						
Opening balance	32,000	14,000				
Sales revenue	15,000	16,000	18,000	20,000	25,000	30,000
Total cash inflow	**15,000**	**16,000**	**18,000**	**20,000**	**25,000**	**30,000**
Cash outflow						
Stock	18,000	16,000	15,000	15,000	16,000	18,000
Wages	3,000	3,000	3,000	3,000	3,000	2,000
Advertising	1,000		1,000		1,000	
Loan repayment	1,000	1,000	1,000	1,000	1,000	1,000
Rent	10,000			10,000		
Total cash outflow	33,000	20,000				
Net cash flow	**(18,000)**	**(4,000)**				
Closing balance	14,000	10,000				

Exam style question

Freepostcodelottery.com

Chris Holbrook, a freelance web developer, launched Freepostcodelottery.com as a free daily lottery draw funded by advertising. He started in 2011 when he had some spare time. He drew the logo, scanned it into a PC, built the website over a weekend and launched. He then went on a few money-saving advice websites and posted information about his new product. This is frowned upon so he had some problems with the websites. However, within a few weeks the idea was reaching people. The visitor numbers were going up.

With this approach, Chris risked very little other than his time. He did very little marketing and used no external finance. He tries to come across as a nice guy rather than a faceless corporation. A lot of interest has come from positive word of mouth. He launched on 1st April 2011 and hit a thousand registrations on 11th May that year. Initially Chris used his own money to fund prizes, but he secured enough revenue from advertisers to break-even later in the year. There was a steady increase to 40,000 daily visits by mid-2014.

Initially Chris approached potential advertisers directly, mainly people he knew. They bought very small amounts of advertising, a few hundred pounds here and there. Then he switched to Google Adsense. Google is good at knowing about people and putting the right ads in front of the right person. Chris just has to specify the parts of his page which would be adverts, and Google does the rest. Google's revenue from Adsense is estimated at over $3bn per quarter, nearly a quarter of Google's total revenue. Revenue for Chris depends on his page's visitor numbers, and is still relatively modest.

Questions

1. What is meant by marketing? *(2 marks)*

2. What is meant by external finance? *(2 marks)*

3. Explain how unlimited liability could affect Chris. *(4 marks)*

4. Calculate an estimate of Google's total annual revenue from the information given, and comment briefly on the value of Adsense to Google. *(4 marks)*

5. Assess the case for Chris using external finance to fund marketing when this lottery was launched. *(8 marks)*

6. Online businesses often have low start-up costs. Assess the value of a business plan for a start-up such as Freepostcodelottery.com. *(10 marks)*

Chapter 5

Sales forecasting
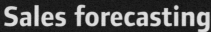
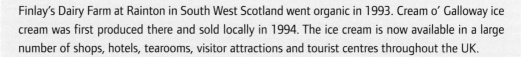

Finlay's Dairy Farm at Rainton in South West Scotland went organic in 1993. Cream o' Galloway ice cream was first produced there and sold locally in 1994. The ice cream is now available in a large number of shops, hotels, tearooms, visitor attractions and tourist centres throughout the UK.

Questions

1. Why would a sales forecast be useful to Cream o' Galloway?

2. How accurate is such a forecast likely to be?

3. Why should ice cream makers pay particular attention to long range weather forecasts?

"Sales forecasting is essential. If you don't plan, you can't know where you're heading. And if you don't know where you're heading, you shouldn't be surprised if you end up nowhere."

Geoff Hurst, marketing director at the Chartered Institute of Marketing

> A **sales forecast** is an estimation of future sales that may be based on previous sales figures, market surveys and trends or managerial estimates.

Purpose of sales forecasts

Sales forecasting is an important part of the financial planning of a business. It's a business tool that uses past and current sales statistics to intelligently predict future levels of sales. An established firm should have a historical record of sales over time to start from. This time series data can help to identify trends and cyclical patterns. Market intelligence can be gathered by the firm or bought from specialist providers.

> **Market intelligence** is information relevant to a company's markets, gathered and analysed specifically to inform accurate and confident decision-making.

Of course, new and start-up businesses cannot make use of past sales data but they can use market research and any related experience to get started. Revenue in a cash flow forecast depends on sales, so it is important for every business to have the best data it can on likely sales.

Sales forecast data is used in many decisions made by managers in areas such as Finance, Strategic management, Operations and Marketing. These decisions may include budgeting, cash flow, expansion, investments in capital equipment, raw materials purchases, inventory management, product positioning and placement, production planning and scheduling, and HR planning for staffing and hiring.

Demand for some products is relatively steady and predictable. To an extent this makes sales forecasts less important for these products. However, even a stable market can have long term trends which could be missed by a sleepy business. Keeping an eye on anything which can influence sales is always useful. For some businesses there are short run variations which make sales forecasts both more difficult and more vital. Ice cream makers, for example, have big peaks in demand when the weather is hot.

> "Ice-cream and lolly sales soared by as much as fourfold in the first two weeks of July as the summer weather reached its peak, leaving some shops and suppliers short of stock."
>
> *The Guardian*, 29 July 2013

An accurate sales forecast means that a business can plan for the future. If the sales forecast uses data saying that during December, in the run-up to Christmas, a business makes 30% of its annual sales, this has implications for the management. They will need to plan production in advance and make sure that they have sufficient inventory on hand to cope with that level of demand. In turn that may mean that cash flow will need watching as the supplies needed to produce the required output may need paying for before revenues from December's sales reach the business. It might also be the signal to increase the level of advertising to maximise sales at this busy time. Extra workers may be needed and more deliveries planned for.

Conversely, if the sales forecast is predicting a seasonal fall in sales, (for many businesses January and February are quiet times after the Christmas rush), then different problems arise and a firm must be ready to make adjustments.

Sales forecasts are also an important part of starting a new business. New businesses need loans or start-up capital to purchase everything necessary to get off the ground and perhaps to finance poor cash flow as sales struggle to begin with. As we saw in Chapter 2, a lender will need to see a business plan to convince them that the business is viable. A central part of that business plan will be the sales forecast. Since there can't be any past sales numbers to use, the business will have to use research about related businesses that have a similar customer base. Any figures produced by this method will need to be adjusted to take into account the difficulty of getting a new product or service on to the market. Many start-up entrepreneurs turn unrealistic hopes into excess optimism.

Sales forecasts are also an invaluable tool when looking backwards in time. Actual sales figures can then be compared with the predicted sales figures and lessons can be learned. The difference between the two figures is called a variance (see page 34). If the actual figures fell short of the predicted level, a negative variance, then managers will want to know why. It may be that the pricing was too high, a rival product may have been launched, advertising and promotion may not have been effective enough or there may have been a problem in the supply chain. Whatever the cause, it needs identification and a remedy. If the actual figures turn out to be higher than predicted, a positive variance, managers may still need to take action. Higher sales may mean that stocks are running low and production may need to be increased.

Sales forecasts play a crucial role in other areas of business management such as managing working capital (later in the book) and in helping to prepare the cash flow forecast that we saw in the last chapter.

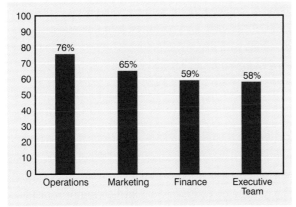

Figure 5.1: Business areas that use sales forecast information

Survey results of 274 manufacturing executives by RBI Interactive research group
Source: RBInteractive Research Group on behalf of Right90, Inc.

Factors affecting sales forecasts

Consumer trends – Unfortunately for many businesses, consumers are not necessarily logical or predictable. Fashions and trends come and go, new products arrive all the time and customer loyalty can be fragile. Just because a product sold well one year does not mean it will continue to do so in the next year. Ultimately it is the consumer that decides the sales figures for a business, marketing may influence consumers to buy your product but you can't make them.

Increasingly, forecasts are guided by the mass of 'big data' available to firms. There are programmes to track user behaviour, such as 'Mixpanel'. This gives detail on what users are doing on the web and mobile devices. Content scoring (e.g. from Kapost) uses technology to tie sales to pieces of marketing content. For example, it could tell how much a single advert added to sales. Predictive modelling crunches data to predict future buyer behaviour. The Lattice Engines version is used by Paypal, for example. The forecasting of consumer trends has become better informed for firms which can access such data.

> **Big data** is high-volume, high-velocity and high-variety information that combines with cost-effective, innovative information processing for better insight and decision making.

Economic variables

The condition of the overall economy often influences the rate of growth (or decline) for particular markets and firms. Individual economic trends will affect different businesses and their sales forecasts in different ways. During the recent recession and downturn, some businesses struggled due to income elastic demand for their products or services, such as travel agents or designer clothes. Conversely some businesses have thrived, with sales figures exceeding their forecasts because they provide cheaper and more attractive alternatives for hard pressed consumers. The discount supermarkets Aldi and Lidl, and Domino's Pizza, are good examples of this.

When there is inflation consumers may buy less of certain goods and services, if their incomes do not keep up with prices. Inflation also creates uncertainty, making consumers cautious and outcomes much harder to predict, prices rise due to inflation but it is hard to quantify the extent to which this will affect sales. An appreciation of the pound can make exported goods more expensive for foreign buyers and cause a fall in sales. Government regulations can increase the price of a product and affect sales, e.g. higher vehicle excise duty on more polluting cars. It can work the other way too; subsidies for installing solar panels have greatly increased their sales.

Such economic variables are outside the control of individual firms but can have a major influence on their performance. To the extent that changes can be predicted, they can be built into sales forecasts. For example, the Governor of the Bank of England (Mark Carney) announced in mid-July 2015 that interest rates were likely to rise by the end of the year. This could result in dearer mortgages reducing spending power in millions of households. Firms with expensive products, which consumers often borrow to buy, might have to cut sales forecasts if borrowing is to become dearer.

Actions of competitors

Nearly all businesses face competition in the market and rivals will strive to maintain their position and if possible take market share away from each other. If one business begins a strong marketing campaign with effective promotion it can lure customers away. Another rival might respond by cutting prices and possibly starting a 'price war'. Two rivals might merge and gain combined strength. Sometimes firms seem to feel that intense competition might harm them all, so the market is relatively calm. However, this is unlikely to go on for ever.

A rival launching a new product that may be better or more innovative is going to affect the sales of existing products. Think, for example, of the impact made by successive new models of smartphone. This makes forecasting tricky as competitors are unlikely to give advance warning of their plans. Imagine the advantage which will go to the first car maker to improve batteries to the point where electric cars can match petrol for performance.

A firm knows its own plans but would be foolish to dismiss the possibility that rivals will somehow steal some competitive advantage – unless the firm has accurate industrial espionage giving details of what others are doing. Without such information they should be careful of predicting sales levels which involve a big increase in their market share.

Businesses in York cannot know when flooding will affect sales.

Difficulties of sales forecasting

Sales forecasts can be compiled from previous data; there are statistical tools that can project trends into the future based on past data. Of course that assumes that the same circumstances and influences that shaped past sales figures will be maintained into the future. As we have seen, customers, economic variables and competitors do not stay constant, their behaviour will change and that will affect the accuracy of the forecast. Despite this, past data can be a useful guide and starting point, experienced managers and analysts may be able to adjust these figures by adjusting for what market intelligence tells them.

For new ventures and products the task is most difficult, as without historical data to work from a forecast has to be done from scratch. Market research will help, as any new product should have had some research done on its likely appeal to consumers. Results from focus groups, product trials and test marketing can be extrapolated to give some idea of sales on a wider basis. Once again, managers can add in their best analysis of how other variables might affect sales and from all of this a forecast can be produced.

Inevitably this is open to error, results from a small test sample will not be replicated by the whole market, and even the most experienced manager cannot predict or make allowances for all future events. Shocks such as natural disasters or a terrorist attack can make nonsense of sales forecasts for many firms. Malaysian Airlines, for example, first lost one plane in mysterious circumstances in 2014 and then had another shot down by Ukrainian rebels. Their sales forecasts suddenly became very unrealistic as people's confidence in them was undermined. Like all future estimates, the further into the future a sales forecast is projected the less accurate it becomes. This makes accurate sales forecasting very difficult indeed for the medium and long term. Nevertheless, sales forecasts are an extremely useful tool, and a necessity in many situations, so managers strive to get the best possible estimates.

Chapter 6

Sales, revenue and costs

TerraCycle

TerraCycle is a recycling and upcycling business which aims to find waste and turn it into something useful, for a profit. Founder Tom Szaky moved from Hungary to Canada and was struck by the mountains of material thrown out in rich communities. Its first activity was collecting organic waste and feeding it to worms, then selling the resulting fertiliser in recycled plastic bottles, as plant food.

Not all activities have been profitable. A bag called the 'reTote', made from

used plastic bags, was sold to a distributor for a few dollars each though the costs were more than $10 per unit. Despite this, the company has grown in 13 years to have revenue of $20m p.a. and 115 employees. It operates in several countries.

Much of the collection of waste materials is now done by volunteers organised in 'brigades'. The volunteers get nothing tangible for themselves but are rewarded by donations to charity and 'a good feeling'. TerraCycle now make few products themselves. They collect the waste and design products and processes. Others are then licensed to make, market and sell the products.

Questions

1. What costs are likely to have contributed to the 'reTote' average of more than $10 per unit?

2. Suggest possible costs to TerraCycle of working with their volunteer waste collection 'brigades'.

3. What are the objectives of TerraCycle?

Put simply, businesses operate by taking *inputs*, changing them in ways that *add value*, and producing *outputs*.

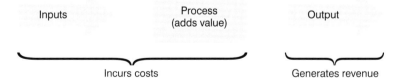

Output (which can be measured by quantity) is sold in order to generate sales revenue (cash income).

Sales are a measure of how many products or services a business sells to its customers. It can be used as a simple description – 'Sales are up this month'. It can be an actual amount – 'Sales volume was 20,000 units this month', or it can be expressed as a monetary value – 'Sales reached £300,000 this month'.

Revenue is the stream of income that is generated by the sale of goods and services. Total Revenue (TR) or sales revenue is used to indicate the total of all revenues earned by a business as many businesses have multiple streams of revenue. It is the top item on an Income statement (profit & loss account).

Costs are the payments that a business makes in order to produce goods and services. They cover a wide variety of payments for inputs such as rent, power, advertising and raw materials. As we shall see below, it is useful to split costs up into different categories.

> The total physical quantity of products sold is the **sales volume**.
>
> The total of incoming receipts for products sold is the **sales revenue**.

Exam tip

Paper 2 will almost certainly include calculations. This is a topic on which calculation questions are common. Plenty of practice to build confidence on these calculations is sensible.

$$\textbf{Sales volume} = \frac{\text{Sales revenue}}{\text{Unit price}} \qquad \text{for example} \quad \frac{£300,000}{£15} = 20,000 \text{ units}$$

Sales revenue is the amount of money gained from the sale of a good or service, it is calculated by…

Sales revenue = Selling price x Sales volume   for example $£15 \times 20,000 = £300,000$

Classifying costs

Fixed costs (**FC**) are not directly affected by how much the business produces. For example, insurance, business rates, rent and loan repayments have to be paid each month regardless of how much has been produced. These costs are not 'fixed' for ever – it is likely that insurance costs will rise if the business makes a claim, for example. It is common for rents and utility charges to increase with inflation. The key issue here is that the level of fixed costs is **not linked to the level of output**. A rising level of output will not immediately affect the fixed costs of a business.

NB: Fixed costs are only fixed in the short term, over a longer period of time they may well change; rents are reviewed and may rise and business rates may be increased by the council and so on. However, for our purposes at the moment, fixed costs are fixed!

Variable costs are **directly linked to the level of output** of a business. They are the costs of resources used to produce units of output, or to deliver a service. They include raw materials and packaging. If the level of output rises, total variable costs will also increase.

A problem to treat carefully

Some costs will not always fit neatly into these two categories. Labour is the obvious example and it all depends on the context. A manager or an office worker will be paid a salary, a regular amount per year split into 12 monthly payments. It does not matter if the business they are employed by is busy or not, their salaries will stay the same. So their labour is a fixed cost. Now consider workers on a zero-hours contract, who only work and get paid when they are needed by the business. If the business is busy they will use more labour, and if the business is quiet they might get no work. The cost of zero-hours labour is directly related to output and so is a variable cost.

To confuse things even further some labour can be considered a bit of both. Many workers are permanently employed for a standard week and so their cost could be considered to be fixed. If they work overtime when the firm needs extra output, their cost will rise. Sometimes the reverse can be true, as they might be asked to work just a three-day week if demand slumps. Both Nissan and Honda did this in response to the crisis from 2008. In this case the cost of labour is related to the level of output, but does not vary directly with output so is semi-fixed or even semi-variable!

TerraCycle's labour costs are low when volunteers collect materials but most of the 115 employees are on fixed salaries. Variable costs for Terracycle include everything directly linked to sorting and processing the waste to prepare it for reuse.

Fixed costs are not directly linked to the level of output of the business. They do not change when output increases or decreases. These are sometimes called indirect costs or overheads. Fixed costs include all loan repayments and interest, but also some regular costs such as staff salaries.

Variable costs are directly linked to the level of output of the business. They change as output increases or decreases. These are sometimes called direct costs. They include materials and the cost of paying any employees paid solely according to their contribution to actual production.

Frank Colzie has just opened a new shop in Bristol which provides a specialist 'one stop' shop for servicing, renovating and buying new and used bikes. Re-Cycle Bristol also offers a full repair and maintenance service.

Make a list of all the costs that Frank would have to pay.

Which fixed costs will have to be paid regardless of whether his shop is active or not?

Which variable costs will depend on how many bikes he sells or repairs?

When we add fixed and variable costs together, they make the total cost for any time period. If we divide total cost by output, that gives us average cost.

Total Cost (TC) = Total Fixed Costs (TFC) + Total Variable Costs (TVC)

Average Variable Cost (AVC) = Total Variable Costs (TVC) ÷ Output (Q)

Average Fixed Cost (AFC) = Total Fixed Costs (TFC) ÷ Output (Q)

Average Total Cost (ATC) = Total Costs (TC) ÷ Output (Q)

Note that **ATC** is often written just as **AC**.

At low levels of output, fixed costs are being shared between fewer units, which might put average costs up. When a firm gets close to capacity output there are likely to be bottlenecks and delays which push up variable costs and eventually average total cost. For most purposes though, we simply treat variable costs as the same per unit, whatever the output level.

Hairdresser Stephanie has fixed costs of £2,000 per month and variable costs of £5 per customer.

If her salon has 100 customers in a month, TC = £2,000 + (100 x 5) = £2,500.

ATC = £2,500/100 = £25.

With 400 customers per month, TC = £2,000 + (400 x 5) = £4,000.

ATC = £4,000/400 = £10.

Like most business owners, Stephanie prefers the salon to stay busy.

Profit is the difference between the value of the total sales revenue of a business and the total costs involved in producing that output. It is Total Revenue minus Total Costs, TR – TC.

Of course, if Total Revenue is less than Total Costs, a loss will be made. In business documents losses are placed in brackets. For example, a £2,000 loss would be shown as (£2,000).

Activity

A dairy farmer makes his own ice cream, each tub of ice cream sells for £4.50. The farmer estimates that the fixed costs each month will be £1,200, the VC of each tub will be £3.00. His sales for the month of June are 1,000 tubs of ice cream.

How much profit will he make in June?

What will happen if it rains a lot and he only sells 600 tubs?

Exam style question

Peter Huan

Peter is a self-employed taxi driver in Kuala Lumpur (Malaysia). He used savings and borrowed from a bank to buy and equip his taxi. His $12,000 loan costs 10% interest per year. On average he works for ten hours per day, mainly splitting those hours between mornings and evenings to work when demand is higher. His monthly costs (typically) are as shown in the table below. Some of these are fixed costs and others depend on how much business he does.

Monthly cost	$
Loan interest	?
Petrol	400
Insurance	80
Advertising	30
Telephone charges	40

Questions

1. What is meant by fixed costs? *(2 marks)*

2. Calculate Peter's monthly loan interest payment. *(2 marks)*

3. Give an example of a variable cost from the table and explain why it is variable. *(4 marks)*

4. Peter's revenue in October was $1,700. Calculate his total cost and his income (profit) for the month. *(4 marks)*

5. Assess the effects on Peter's ATC and profit if he is busier in the next month. *(8 marks)*

6. Assess the likely impact on costs and revenue of employing a second driver to add to the hours for which the taxi is working. *(10 marks)*

Chapter 7

Break-even

Selling memory

Kelvin has become a part-time eBay trader, slowly building up his business. He sold a few unwanted items from home and then his CDs (which he first stored electronically). Now he specialises in novelty usb memory sticks, in moulded plastic shapes such as cartoon characters or guitars. He started selling these using the eBay 'buy it now' system with a fixed price, generally around £6. Now he uses a combined approach, auctioning with no reserve price but also including a 'buy it now' option.

He buys in bulk from Hong Kong at an average total cost around £3.50 (excluding onward postage for which he adds a charge). Sometimes his auctioned items sell at low prices, but he doesn't see this as a problem. He finds that low initial bids for auctioned items attract buyers to his sale. Many of these buyers are either impatient or fear not winning at auction. As a result, he sells more 'buy it now' items at £6 than he did when not offering the auction option. This business takes up an hour or two most evenings and he makes daily trips to the post office. Kelvin has reached the point where he is thinking about giving up his main job, adding more products, and becoming a full-time trader.

Questions

1. What risks are involved in Kevin's business?

2. Should he count his own time as a cost?

3. Why might he be tempted to become a full-time trader?

Contribution: selling price – variable cost per unit

Contribution is an extremely useful concept; it is the difference between the selling price of a product and its variable costs **P – AVC**. (It is more often written as P – VC.)

By subtracting the AVC from the unit price the direct costs of producing each item are covered. This does not mean that the amount left is profit; fixed costs still need to be paid. So each time a unit is sold, that amount, the contribution, is available to help pay off the fixed costs. Once the fixed costs have been paid off by all the individual contributions, extra sales will now contribute to profit.

Living with his parents allows Kelvin to see everything he gets above £3.50 for a memory stick as profit. If he went full-time he would have to rent premises, perhaps on a local business park. His research suggests that he would then have fixed costs of around £500 per week. Using the unit cost and price shown above (price £6 and £3.50 AVC) is a simplification because his range of products would increase, but it is a useful simplification. On a typical sale, the £2.50 left after paying the variable cost would be a contribution towards either meeting fixed costs or to profit.

> **Contribution** is the amount each sale provides towards fixed costs or profit. Price – VC.

The break-even point

If he went full-time, Kelvin would need to sell 200 memory sticks per week just to cover his fixed costs (as 200 x £2.50 = £500). If he took a week off and sold nothing, he would lose £500 that week. Once sales go above 200 per week, he would make profits. This means that 200 sales per week would be his **break-even point**. His position would be as shown below:

Sales	Costs and Revenue	Outcome
Zero	Fixed costs only, Revenue zero	Loss (£500)
Below break-even (1-199)	Fixed costs + variable costs > Revenue	Smaller loss
Break-even (200)	Fixed costs + variable costs = Revenue	No loss, no profit
Above break-even >200	Fixed costs + variable costs < Revenue	Profits made

Kelvin also has regular auction sales at variable prices. When an auctioned memory stick sells at above £3.50, it makes a contribution – but sometimes a small one. Only on sales below £3.50 does he make a loss.

Returning to the dairy farmer who makes his own ice cream, mentioned in the last chapter, each tub of ice cream sells for £4.50. The farmer calculates that the fixed costs each month will be £1,200, the VC of each tub are £3.00.

His monthly break-even point will be…

$$BEP = \frac{FC}{Contribution\ (P - VC)} \qquad \frac{£1,200}{(£4.50 - £3.00)} \qquad \frac{£1,200}{£1.50} = 800\ tubs$$

After a wet June, the farmer decides to reduce the price. His freezers are full and he needs to sell more in order to use the milk he is producing. He decides to reduce the price to £4.

What will happen to the contribution figure?

How will this affect the break-even point?

What will have to happen to make the break-even point achievable?

How promising do you think this business looks?

The Break Even Point (BEP) is the level of output at which Total Revenue is exactly the same as Total Costs. At this point, neither a profit nor a loss is being made. **TR = TC**. When sales are **above** the break-even point the business will make a **profit**. When sales are **below** the break-even point the business will make a **loss**.

$$BEP = \frac{FIXED\ COSTS}{CONTRIBUTION} \quad or \quad \frac{FIXED\ COSTS}{(SP - VC)}$$

(SP above is selling price, VC is average variable cost)

⚠ WATCH OUT!

Although these calculations use money values, the result they give is a quantity of output (needed to reach break-even revenue).

This is an important concept for any business, particularly for new businesses. Break-even analysis means looking at the break-even point and deciding if the business venture will be feasible. Different prices and costs can be considered to see how the BEP changes, and profit levels can be worked out over a range of outputs. Break-even analysis will be a key element in most business plans.

Margin of safety

At any level of sales above the BEP, a business is profitable. There is a number of units by which sales volume can fall before reaching the BEP, known as the **margin of safety**. The larger the margin of safety, the greater a fall in sales the business can absorb before making a loss. The business shown below has sales of 2,200, a BE point at 1,000 units and so a margin of safety of 2,200 – 1,000 = 1,200 units. Generally, the greater the margin of safety the better position a business is in. This looks to be a good margin of safety.

Figure 7.1: Break-even chart for a profitable business

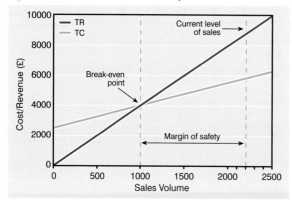

The green cost line (above) starts at above zero because there are fixed costs even when output is zero. The red revenue line goes up more steeply because the price per unit is above the variable costs – otherwise there would be no chance of profit.

> ### Activity
>
> Construct a break-even chart for Kelvin if his full-time business sells 300 memory sticks per week.

Interpretation of break-even charts

A break-even chart also gives us another way of finding the break-even point. In the diagram above, we can see that this is at 1,000 units sold because this is where TR = TC. Realistically, firms would not sit down with a ruler and paper as their preferred method of calculation. However, the chart gives a quick guide to break-even and to the margin of safety. Being able to interpret such a chart is important. Another way to look at the chart is as a picture of how much sales can fall before the business makes a loss. The value of break-even analysis and charts is that they can:

Inform pricing decisions – A business may calculate the break-even level of sales at a range of different prices as a way of helping to decide how much to charge for a product or service. It will want to be confident that predicted sales volumes will allow the business to make enough profit, bearing in mind potential demand.

Predict profit – If a business is in a competitive situation it may have to accept the market price, with no real choice about the price they charge. They may, therefore, use BE analysis as a tool to predict how much profit they are likely to make at different volumes of sales.

Seek finance – Investors and lenders will only commit money to a business idea if they are confident that it will be profitable. BE analysis can form part of a *business plan*. This is a document used to promote a business idea to potential investors or lenders.

Conduct 'what-if' analysis – Businesses may want to 'model' the impact of changes, such as changing price (see above) or to forecast the impact of possible changes in demand, or in fixed or variable costs. BE analysis allows such changes to be included in a BE calculation so that new BE levels can be identified. If

Charts and graphs give valuable illustrations but businesses rely on numbers.

demand (or total sales) is forecast to change, BE analysis can focus on the margin of safety and whether the business is likely to remain profitable.

Limitations of break-even analysis

BE analysis assumes that fixed and variable costs are known. Especially during business planning, an entrepreneur may have to make a 'best guess' at costs. The analysis assumes that variable costs rise steadily in proportion to output, but they may not; economies of scale such as bulk buying can reduce the cost per unit. Hence, the quality of BE analysis will depend on the accuracy of the assumptions made about future costs.

Estimates of sales and revenue made using market research will be based on evidence from before pricing decisions are made. In a dynamic economy there are many variables that could change during the time lag between research and final decisions. For example, consumer tastes and incomes, resource costs and competitor innovations can change the situation, either individually or in some combination. Alertness and readiness to modify assumptions can help, but it can become necessary to go back to square one.

Where prices fluctuate frequently, or different prices are charged for the same product, BE analysis needs simplifying assumptions about pricing as well as about costs. Think, for example, of Kelvin's mix of 'buy it now' and auction sales. It is dangerously easy to make optimistic assumptions in such a situation.

BE analysis identifies total revenue and profit at different sales volumes. However, it doesn't guarantee that a business will generate sufficient demand to sell at this level. A business needs to be able to judge the likely demand for a product accurately (as well as costs) to calculate BE data. BE analysis can highlight the need to market the product more effectively in order to reach the sales volume needed to cover costs.

The biggest danger is that BE figures based on over optimistic assumptions about costs or/and revenue will produce misleading data. Firms might stick to plans based on false expectations, expecting reality to mirror their first estimates. A careful firm will keep a questioning attitude and be prepared to modify their analysis as soon as events and evidence show limitations in their data. Ideally, BE analysis should be seen as a valuable starting point rather than something which produces final answers.

Chapter 8

Budgets

Selling jewellery

Mary Lewis produced her hand-made jewellery using African designs. She sold it in three categories (bracelets, earrings and necklaces), some on market stalls but more and more via retail outlets. In her second year of business she drew up a sales budget for her designs.

Sales Budget	October	November	December
Bracelets	£200	£300	£500
Earrings	£160	£320	£480
Necklaces	£225	£375	£750

Mary was in her second year of business when she prepared these budgets. The months before Christmas were her best months the previous year but she now supplied her goods to retail outlets and was never sure how much promotion the retailer would give. Mary's margins on jewellery sold in shops were lower as the shopkeeper had to be paid. She anticipated that in the run up to Christmas sales would be split 50/50 between her market stall and craft fairs on the one hand, and retail outlets on the other. Whilst her stalls took cash, she expected a month's delay before revenue from retailers would arrive.

Questions

1. Mary's sales budget was based on historical information. What does this mean?
2. How might a sales budget help Mary?

Break-even analysis is clearer if we stick to just one product. In reality, many firms have a more complicated mix of revenue and cost streams. Budgets help firms keep tabs on these streams.

> A **budget** is a financial plan for the future that sets out targets to be met, the costs of achieving them and how that spending might be financed.

A forecast looks very similar to a budget and the mechanics of putting a forecast together are the same as for a budget. However a forecast has a different emphasis from a budget, a forecast allows the business to look into the future and is a realistic expectation of what is likely to happen. By contrast, a budget targets what the business would like to happen. Instead of telling you where you want to go, which is what your budget does, forecasts tell you where you are probably going.

Purpose of budgets

A business may use a budget in different contexts such as sales revenue, production costs, overheads, personnel, cash, capital expenditure and expected profit. Each budget can be used for more than one purpose, and the main purposes are summarised below. It is a guide to managers and staff as to what they are expected to achieve over a certain time period. For example, this may mean reaching a certain level of sales revenue or not spending more on costs than the sum allowed. A major purpose of a budget is to help control expenditure by focusing on costs and to increase revenues by focusing on sales. This should ideally result in the business maximising its profits.

Purpose	Description
Planning	Preparation of budget information will enable a firm to plan its cash flow and to regulate spending. Waste and inefficiency might be identified by budgets. Managers can identify areas of income and expenditure which they have potential problems with and/or should pay particular attention to.
Forecasting	Target budgets can be put alongside forecasts to see how realistic expectations are and to modify both budgets and forecasts as necessary.
Communication	Co-ordination between departments should improve if everyone is working to the same budget. People with delegated power should have a clear picture of what is expected from budget information.
Motivation	A budget should provide clear targets on costs and sales for everyone, strengthening their sense of purpose and increasing job satisfaction when budget targets are met.

Figure 8.1: The budget process

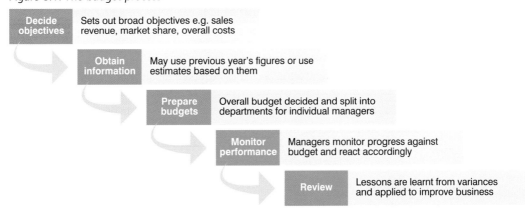

Budgets are normally set for 12 months and coincide with the accounting year, although they can be for much shorter periods of time. Senior management will devise an overall budget and budgets for individual departments; then it is up to departmental managers to implement them. Budgets act as a form of supervision and departmental managers are expected to stick to the targets set out in the budget. If managers wish to vary the targets, they must be able to justify it to senior management. After the time period is up the actual figures can be compared to the planned budget and the performance of the department can be reviewed. The difference between a budget and the actual outcome is called a variance.

Historical figures

Existing businesses most often produce a budget based on historical figures, such as last year's sales levels and costs. This gives a basis on which to model the next year's targets. This approach is basically **extrapolation**. A review of the historical figures is useful first, to identify concerns or areas for improvement. In other words, the firm can learn lessons from past experience. Costs may have increased by more than was budgeted for due to unavoidable reasons, as inflation may have pushed up the price of inputs. In such a case, the new budget may be altered to reflect this and perhaps allow for continued inflation or for other expected changes. The advantage of using historical figures is that they are real experience and reasonably straightforward and can be adapted to fulfil the aims of the business. For example the sales revenue target may be based on last year's figures but with an added 10% to reflect a desire for more market share.

> A **historical** approach to budgeting starts from the recorded experience of previous years. **Extrapolation** means assuming that past trends will continue into the future. This is not guaranteed to happen but is often the best starting point.

A new business has no historical figures on which to base a budget. It can start by estimating all costs and revenues and hoping they are somewhere near to what will happen. Or, they can use a zero based approach. After the first year they can decide whether to follow the historical budgeting method or carry on with the zero based approach.

Zero based

Zero based budgeting means starting from scratch each year with no money allocated to cover costs. Managers have to estimate the budget that they will need to do their job. They will then need to be prepared to bid for and justify that level of spending to senior management. They may or may not be successful in their bids.

In theory this allocates resources more efficiently as managers have to think and plan more carefully knowing that they will have to get agreement from above. It may be easier to adapt a zero based budget as circumstances change. On the other hand it can be more time consuming and expensive, forceful managers may be more successful in attracting funds than others who may have more worthwhile projects.

Some businesses may use a mixture of the two systems to get the best of both worlds i.e. departments receive a 'base' budget and are expected to negotiate for any additions.

> **Zero based** budgets start with no assumptions based on experience. Managers are asked to bid for funds or predict revenue they can raise. Then they negotiate an agreed budget.

Variance analysis

A variance indicates how the business is performing against its budgets. A favourable variance means that the actual figures are 'better' than the planned ones. An adverse variance means that the actual figures are 'worse' than the planned ones. A variance means that the business has not been completely accurate with its original budget, something has not matched expectations.

Figure 8.2: Adverse and favourable variances

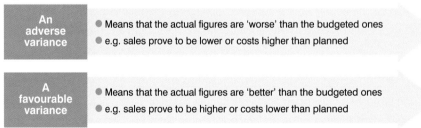

> A **variance** is the difference between a budgeted figure and the actual figure.

It is useful to investigate adverse (negative) variances to find out why they have happened and to quickly put things right if something has gone wrong. Delays could allow things to get worse. An adverse variance on costs can mean that profitability is compromised; the business should find out why costs have gone beyond their planned maximum so they can get them back under control. Although at first glance a favourable variance sounds like good news, this is not necessarily the case. It may indicate that the business isn't being stretched enough or could have made more of its opportunities.

Small variances are not a major problem; staff can actually be motivated by small variances. An adverse one can encourage them to close the gap and a favourable one to feel satisfied. On the other hand a large variance is a problem; it can cause feelings of complacency if it is a favourable one, or it can be de-motivating if it is an adverse one. Staff might feel disheartened and that they have no chance of catching up.

Mike Elliot specialises in the repair of Alpha Romeo cars.

| | March | | April | | May | |
	Budget £	Actual £	Budget £	Actual £	Budget £	Actual £
Wages	2,000	2,000	2,000	2,000	2,000	2,000
Materials	1,250	1,000	1,250	1,300	1,250	1,450
Advertising	100	100	100	100	100	125
Motor expenses	250	300	250	325	250	350
Other overheads	200	175	200	170	200	180
Total Costs	**3,800**	**3,575**	**3,800**	**3,895**	**3,800**	**4,105**

Questions

1. Calculate the total cost variance for the 3 month period.

2. Is this variance favourable or adverse? Explain your answer.

3. Why do you think the budgeted and actual figures for wages are identical?

4. Identify an example of a favourable variance and an adverse variance from the figures provided.

5. The actual figure for 'materials' is different each month. Outline possible reasons for this.

6. Should Mike Elliot be concerned by the variances shown?

Difficulties of budgeting

Budgeting is not that easy to get right. Historical figures are not always completely reliable. Basing a budget on previous figures assumes that business conditions remain unchanged or stay similar, and of course they do not. Sales figures can be affected by many variables (some of these were discussed in the section on sales forecasts), the same applies to costs. For example, energy and fuel costs are notoriously unpredictable, commodity prices are volatile. Economic variables such as exchange rates and inflation can affect both costs and revenues. Governments can change the levels of taxation, which will affect consumers via their disposable incomes and willingness to spend. New regulations can alter the market, such as European directives or consumer protection laws. The economy is

Energy and fuel costs are notoriously unpredictable.

dynamic and is affected by the business cycle; sales may be slowed by the downturn and recessionary phases. Complacency about budget figures is dangerous.

As a product moves through its life cycle, it places different demands on budgets, for example less advertising may be needed. On top of all this, businesses have to try to take into account what their competitors might do.

Then there are decisions to be made about the direction the business is heading in. If the business wishes to expand, how much extra should be added to sales targets? If the business has grown by say, 15% in the previous year, is this going to be a realistic target again? Coming up with realistic and accurate budget targets is not an easy thing to do.

Exam style question

Windermere Lake Cruises

Windermere Lake Cruises in Cumbria has 15 boats of varying sizes and is one of the top 10 paid-for tourist attractions in the UK. It is also a big local employer with up to 170 staff in the summer and 100 or so in the off-season.

In 2011 it carried 1.3 million passengers. In early 2012 the recession and the nationwide bad weather meant that passenger numbers were down by 10%. During July, in the run-up to the Olympics, numbers were down by 22% and groups of foreign visitors dropped by 38% in August. The area gets a lot of visitors from China and Japan. Their general routes start in London. With the Olympics taking place, hotels were very expensive, so it meant tours were cancelled. Coach tours to the Lake District were cancelled because of the demand to take coaches to London to transport Olympic officials.

A spokesman said "There will be fewer jobs and we will have to lay off some people from seasonal jobs a bit earlier, and reconsider our winter maintenance projects to see what we can afford."

Question

Evaluate the importance of Windermere Cruises preparing a budget for 2012.   *(20 marks)*

Chapter 9

Profit

Mr Micawber's famous, and oft-quoted, recipe for happiness:

> "Annual income twenty pounds, annual expenditure nineteen, nineteen and six, result happiness. Annual income twenty pounds, annual expenditure twenty pounds, ought and six, result misery."

Charles Dickens, David Copperfield

Question

Why does a firm want more income than expenditure?

Profit can be counted in different ways. The important measures for this unit are **Gross Profit**, **Operating Profit** and **Profit for the year** (**Net profit**). They are all part of the **Statement of comprehensive income** (**profit and loss account**). This, as its name implies, is a financial statement detailing the amount of profit or loss a business has made over a given time period.

When a business receives income from the sale of its products (turnover), it has various items it must pay for (costs) before it can calculate its profits. To complicate things, firms and books can use different terms to describe the same thing. Remember that turnover, sales revenue and total revenue all mean the same thing. Variable costs, direct costs and cost of sales are all terms used to describe costs that vary with the level of output. Fixed costs, indirect costs, overheads and expenses are all terms used to describe costs that do not vary with output in the short term. You might come across all these terms. Be careful with old books, because the way things are counted has changed.

When calculating the different measures of profit it is common to use cost of sales for variable and expenses for fixed costs. Interest and taxes which would normally be treated as expenses are separated from other operating expenses as explained below.

Calculation of gross profit

Gross profit is revenue minus cost of sales. Revenue only includes completed sales (delivered to the customer) during the time period, normally an accounting year. Revenue includes both cash and credit sales.

> **Gross profit = Revenue – Cost of sales**

Although this gives a useful guide, it does not cover other expenses involved in running a business. We have to take it a step further. Businesses need to know how much money is left after all costs have been paid.

Operating profit

Operating profit is calculated by taking away all other operating expenses such as salaries, rent and advertising. It is the profit earned from the normal or everyday operation of the business.

> **Operating profit = Gross profit – other operating expenses**

It is also known by the acronym EBIT (Earnings Before Interest and Taxes) and as operating income. This does not include any profit from investments or the effects of interest and taxes.

Operating profit is a good indicator of how well the business is doing. It is watched closely by all stakeholders, because it shows both the demand for the business' products or services in terms of sales, and the efficiency of production as measured by its costs. Interest and taxes are left out because they are beyond the control of the business. Interest costs depend on how the business is financed (with debt or equity) and can be influenced by interest rates.

Profit for the year (net profit)

Profit for the year is the bottom line of the income statement. It is the amount of profit that goes to owners of the business. They may re-invest it or distribute it amongst the owners/shareholders. It is what is left over from revenues after all costs and expenses are subtracted.

> **Profit for the year = Operating profit – Tax and interest**

Profit for the year, net profit, net income, and net earnings all mean the same thing.

Figure 9.1: The stages of the Income Statement

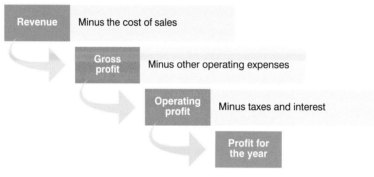

Activity

Apple's financial results for the three months ended on 28 March 2015 (in $m) were:

Revenue $58,010, cost of sales $34,354, other operating expenses $5,378 and interest, tax and other non-operational expenses $4,995.

Calculate the gross profit, operating profit and the profit for the quarter (net profit).

Statement of comprehensive income (profit and loss account)

The Income Statement is a financial document measuring the financial performance of a business and summarising its transactions over a specified period, usually a year or a quarter. It is often referred to as a profit and loss statement (P&L).

This is a most important document, used by accountants and business owners (the second main document is the Statement of Financial Position or Balance Sheet – in the next chapter). It shows how revenue is converted into a profit or a loss over the year or quarter. There is a contrast between an Income Statement which represents a period of time and a Statement of Financial Position which represents a single moment in time. This is like the difference between measuring a flow of water into a bath (in a time period) and the amount of water in the bath (at one moment).

There is no fixed format for the Income Statement and some businesses will show different items and categories from others. At first glance they can appear daunting but they all have the same basic idea. In essence they are just a large take-away sum, starting with a big pile of money and then taking away all the various costs and expenditures until the final profit (or loss) for the year is left.

Income statement for Jaguar Land Rover for year ended 31st March 2015

	2015 £m	2014 £m	Change £m
Revenue	21,866	19,386	2,480
Cost of sales	(13,185)	(11,904)	(1,281)
Gross profit	**8,681**	**7,482**	**1,199**
Employees	(1,977)	(1,654)	(323)
Other operating expenses	(2,572)	(2,435)	
Operating profit	**4,132**	**3,393**	**739**
Interest and non-operational expenses	(1,518)	(892)	
Tax	(576)	(622)	46
Profit for year	**2,038**	**1,879**	**159**

This income statement for Jaguar Land Rover has been simplified, but it shows the stages described above. It also shows the previous financial year's figures for comparison. Some accounts may show the figures for up to five previous financial years.

Calculation of gross, operating and net profit margins

Profitability describes the ability of a business to generate profits from its resources.

We can see that Jaguar Land Rover has increased the amount of profit for the year between 2014 and 2015 by £159m, but we can't tell if profitability has improved without an extra step. We can measure profitability by using a profit margin, which is an example of a financial ratio (a figure calculated from other figures to give useful information to business managers).

Jaguar Land Rover profits rose in 2015.

> A **profit margin** shows the percentage of turnover that is profit. It is the ratio of profit to turnover expressed as a percentage.

The good news is that it doesn't matter whether you are calculating a gross, operating or net (= profit for the year) margin, the formula is the **same**...

$$\frac{\text{PROFIT}}{\text{TURNOVER}} \times 100 =$$ (the answer will be expressed as a %)

Gross profit margin $\qquad = \dfrac{\text{Gross profit} \times 100}{\text{Turnover}}$

Operating profit margin $\qquad = \dfrac{\text{Operating profit} \times 100}{\text{Turnover}}$

Net = Profit for the year margin $\quad = \dfrac{\text{Profit for the year} \times 100}{\text{Turnover}}$

Below are some Marks and Spencer figures from which we can calculate the operating profit margin:

Marks & Spencer	Financial year 2014-15 (£ million)
Turnover	10,311.4
Operating profit	762.5

$$\frac{\text{Operating profit}}{\text{Turnover}} \times 100 \qquad \frac{762.5 \times 100}{10,311.4} = 7.40\%$$

Should M&S be pleased with this level of operating profit? How useful is a figure like this?

The answer is that by itself a profit margin is not very useful. As with any financial ratio/figure, a profit margin is only meaningful if compared with another figure, either figures for the business from earlier years, or figures from other businesses in a similar situation for the same year.

The operating profit margin for Marks and Spencer of 7.40% does not tell us much by itself, but if we know that for the previous year it was 7.20 %, it puts the figure into perspective and gives us a way of analysing the performance of Marks and Spencer. Knowing that in 2015 the operating profit margin for Walmart was 5.49%, gives us another useful comparison by which to judge the financial performance of Marks and Spencer.

Exam tip

If asked to comment on a ratio, look for something to compare it with when possible.

Managers will use financial information like this to assess how well a business is doing. An increase over previous figures indicates that they are on the right track; a decrease is cause for concern and a signal for action. Even an increase can be a worry if it is less than competitors have achieved.

Operating profit margins vary from industry to industry and also by size. It is acceptable to run a business on a low profit margin if turnover is high. For example supermarkets typically run on a low profit margin of around 5%. This is good if you are Walmart with a turnover of $485.7 billion in 2015, but not so good if you are a small village shop with a turnover of £80,000.

Risky businesses look for higher profit margins. Supermarkets can cope with a low profit margin. They buy enormous quantities of food and other consumer goods. They add value simply by ensuring that stocks are available in a convenient place at convenient times to meet the needs of consumers. Most customers' spending will be fairly stable over time and sudden changes are unlikely. A risky business, like oil, will need a higher profit margin to survive. It has to fund expensive exploration, sometimes finding nothing. Also something may go horribly wrong, as it did for BP in the Gulf of Mexico in 2010.

Activity

Go back to the income statement for Jaguar Land Rover and calculate the gross, operating and profit for the year margins for 2015 and 2014.

What conclusions can you draw about the performance of Jaguar Land Rover?

What else might you want to know?

Ways to improve profitability

Tesco plc

In the financial year ending 28th February 2014, Tesco plc recorded a profit margin for the year of 3.01%. In the same period up to 2015 the position had changed for the worse and Tesco made a loss of (£5,719m) on a turnover of £62,284m.

Calculate the loss for the year margin.

Think of different ways for Tesco to improve its profitability and prevent further losses.

Profitability depends on the relationship between revenue and costs, or the price per unit and the average cost of production. Quite a bit of this course is about ways of improving profits. Many other chapters go into detail on what is below. This section sets out a framework to organise thinking.

Costs can be reduced, prices increased, turnover increased and productivity increased. Any of these will help to generate more profit from the resources available. Which to use will vary depending on the product, the market conditions and the reactions of consumers and competition.

Ways of increasing profitability

Sales – Raising the price will increase the profit made on each unit sold, but is likely to reduce the number sold. The success of this approach depends on the price elasticity of demand for the product. Competition, consumer loyalty and the perception of the brand will influence this. A higher price can signify quality and should be successful if demand is price inelastic. Another idea is to use price segmentation which is based on the fact that different customers are willing to pay different prices. Charging different prices to the different segments can bring substantial increases in profits and profitability. Examples of segmentation include discounts for students or senior citizens, cheaper fares at off-peak times and higher package holiday prices in school holidays.

Figure 9.2: Increasing profitability

If increasing price is too risky it may be possible to boost the quantity sold, this increases profitability as fixed costs are spread over a wider range of output which reduces average total cost. Increasing output may bring economies of scale which can also reduce average costs. This assumes that the business has

Aldi's sales revenue rose by 27.3% in 2014.

spare capacity and that customers will buy more. They may need persuading with extra marketing and promotion, which may be expensive and cancel out any gains in profitability.

> In 2014 Aldi's adverts came top of a study by Marketing magazine. The magazine found Aldi's brand was the most consistently well-recalled throughout the year as a whole. Aldi won despite its adverts being banned twice last year by the Advertising Standards Authority, following complaints by rival supermarket chains. In that same year Aldi's sales revenue increased by 27.3%.

Costs – Reducing costs is the easiest and most obvious way to increase profitability. Reducing direct costs will increase the gross profit margin and reducing overheads will increase the operating profit margin. Monitoring and management of costs is good business practice and involves minimising expenditure. Inputs should have the best balance between profitability and cost. Suppliers should be compared and prices keenly negotiated. The risk is that driving down costs can compromise quality, with an impact on reputation and future sales.

Faulty products and production glitches cause waste, costs and perhaps lost revenue. Improving the standard of production and reducing waste can increase profitability. Energy can be a major cost and energy efficiency can make big contributions to cost saving.

> American courier UPS used computer mapping to re-plan its routes, eliminating as many left turns as possible as trucks wasted fuel waiting to cross the traffic. The fuel saved was enough for 20 million extra miles. Staples office supplies limited its USA trucks to 60mph and saved $8m in fuel costs.

Productivity – Productivity gains mean more output from the same level of inputs. This makes more efficient use of the available resources, and so the average cost of production is reduced. Technology plays a big part here. Computers and complex machinery speed up production, improve quality and in some cases revolutionise processes.

Training can improve the knowledge and skills of staff, boosting output and productivity. Improved recruitment and selection can have the same effect. Better employee motivation can be the most powerful factor of all; schemes that engage and encourage staff can bring major gains in output and quality. It is not just individual pieces of machinery or a person's capability being improved. Successful integration of capital and labour into complex systems can bring big gains in productivity.

> In 2014 Jaguar Land Rover opened its £500m Engine Manufacturing Centre at Wolverhampton, where 150 state-of-the-art machines work across three production lines. Everything from assembly robots and lasers to drilling and high-pressure wash machines operate here. The centre has the largest rooftop solar panel installation in the UK and will generate more than 30 per cent of the site's energy. Its 1500 workers have all received comprehensive training packages.

Distinction between profit and cash

Many businesses have to cease trading because they have run out of cash, even though they could be profitable. Businesses can survive for long periods of time without making a profit, provided they have enough working capital (cash). But they cannot survive for long without cash to pay the bills. We have seen earlier that cash flow management is crucial. Agreeing a sale at a profitable price might involve a wait for payment to be received, whilst costs need urgent settlement.

> **Cash** is usually in the form of money or bank deposits, some businesses would also include assets that can easily be converted into money e.g. finished products.
>
> **Profit** is the difference over a period of time between total sales revenue and total production costs.

Many businesses need to make extensive cash expenditures before they see any reward in the form of profit. A builder is a good example of the difference between long term profitability and the short term need for cash.

Land, building plans, materials, labour, utility connections, contractors and other costs will need paying for months and perhaps even longer. Workers or suppliers will not wait until the house is finished before being paid. The builder needs working capital to cover costs as work progresses. He has to plan outgoings in advance and finance these payments until he sells the house.

Very often profit is a long term prospect. When all the start-up costs of a new business must be paid before sales can take place, significant working capital will be required. Cash can be a short-term problem even if prospects of long-term profitability are good. But if profits do not materialise eventually, the firm is doomed because lenders will not supply endless working capital.

It is not just the waiting for payment to come through that causes cash problems. A business can become a victim of its own success by expanding too quickly. This is called overtrading. New and growing businesses are particularly at risk here. Following a successful launch, orders pour in and the business rushes to fulfil them, only to find that it does not have the working capital to fund the extra supplies/workers/distribution needed. Business failure can follow.

> **Overtrading** happens when a business expands too quickly and tries to take on more business than the working capital will allow.

Chapter 10

Liquidity

"Turnover is vanity, profit is sanity, but cash is reality" – old business adage

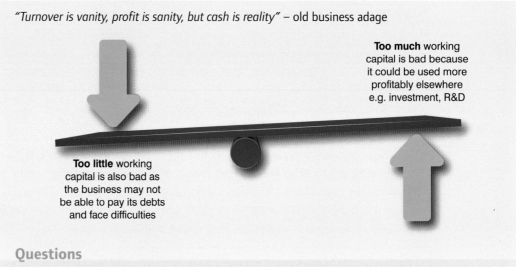

Too much working capital is bad because it could be used more profitably elsewhere e.g. investment, R&D

Too little working capital is also bad as the business may not be able to pay its debts and face difficulties

Questions

1. How is opportunity cost relevant to holding cash in working capital?

2. What advice would you offer to (a) a friend and (b) a business if they are struggling to pay bills?

Liquidity in the business sense refers to how much cash a business has and the ease with which it can pay its debts. If the business is illiquid, it may need more working capital. It may not be able to pay its bills or cover its short term debts. It may become insolvent and have to stop trading.

Statement of financial position (balance sheet)

The **statement of financial position** is one of the key financial documents (along with the income statement) that businesses will prepare and use. Data is normally presented in a vertical column as shown on page 45. Terms used and the detail may vary, but the format is essentially the same.

> The **statement of financial position** shows the assets, liabilities and net worth of a business on a given date. This is also known as the balance sheet.

The statement of financial position gives a 'snapshot' of the assets and liabilities of a business on a particular date and time. In theory, a business could publish a new and different version of the statement of financial position every day, but they generally do so each quarter or perhaps each year. The statement shows what the business owns (assets) and owes (liabilities); the difference is the net worth of the business. It shows where money has gone and where it came from.

> **Assets** include everything that could be of benefit to an organisation. Those that appear on the statement of financial position are the ones that can be given a money value.
>
> **Liabilities** include all debts that must be repaid at some time in the future.

The purpose of the statement of financial position is to give information about the current status of the business on the date it was compiled. This information is used to estimate the liquidity, funding, and debt position of a business, and has the figures for a number of liquidity ratios. These give further useful information to managers and may guide action.

The statement of financial position below shows the basic layout and the meaning of terms used.

Statement of financial position for Skiprigg Ltd as at 18th February 2015 (£)

Total fixed assets	385,000	Total of all fixed assets at *current value*
Inventory	60,000	Materials, semi-finished & finished goods stocks
Debtors	35,000	Money owed *to* the business
Cash	15,000	Cash in the bank and at hand
Total current assets	**110,000**	Stock + debtors + cash
Creditors	50,000	Money owed *by* the business
Total current liabilities	**50,000**	
Net current assets	**60,000**	Current assets – current liabilities
Assets employed	**445,000**	Total fixed assets + net current assets
Long term liabilities	100,000	Loans lasting longer than 1 year
Share capital	240,000	Money invested by the owners
Reserves	105,000	Retained profit
Capital employed	**445,000**	Long term liabilities + share capital + reserves

A feature of a statement of financial position is that ASSETS EMPLOYED = CAPITAL EMPLOYED. This is where its alternative name comes from: the Balance Sheet must always balance. 'Assets employed' shows where the money is used and 'Capital employed' shows where it has come from. This balance is always there, regardless of whether the financial position of the business is good or terrible.

The terms used can vary. Assets employed is sometimes called 'total assets' and capital employed is sometimes 'owner's equity'.

Fixed assets are assets that will be of lasting value to the business. They include land, buildings, machinery and equipment. Capital expenditure means investing in fixed assets. These can include tangible items (land, property, machinery and vehicles) and intangibles such as goodwill, brands and patents. Tangible assets lose value over time (depreciation) so will usually be worth less on the next balance sheet.

Intangible assets have no physical existence; as well as goodwill, brands and patents, they include the technical and managerial experience that the business has developed. Goodwill, brands and patents can be given a money value but the technical and managerial experience cannot. Intangible assets can be very valuable but this may vary over time – e.g. when a patent runs out or if a brand goes out of fashion.

Current assets (inventory, debtors and cash) are assets that the business has for a short period of time. Inventory will be used and then sold. Debtors will pay up. These items will become cash, usually within one year.

Current liabilities are debts that the business will need to pay within a year or less. They can include money owed to creditors, tax that has to be paid, overdrafts and dividends.

Net current assets are current assets minus current liabilities. They are the working capital of the business, which is available to cover everyday spending. Working capital needs careful management; otherwise the business may not be able to pay its short-term debts. On the other hand, too much idle working capital means the business should be using this cash asset elsewhere.

Long term liabilities are long term debts that the business will pay off over several years e.g. mortgages and loans.

Share capital counts as a liability, as does the money put into a business by a sole trader or a partnership (owner's equity). This is because if the business closed they would want their money back, the business is using their money so it is regarded as a debt.

Reserves, including retained profits and gains from increases in asset values such as property, count as a liability because they are a source of finance.

Exam tip

Just trying to learn all this by heart is difficult and can get boring. Firms publish statements of financial position. Find some online for firms you know of, then look at them and ask yourself what each item is. This can quickly build up your understanding and confidence.

Measuring liquidity

A business short of liquidity may not be able to pay its bills. It may become insolvent and have to stop trading. The liquidity of assets varies, depending on how easily they can be turned into cash. Fixed assets such as machinery and factories are not very liquid. If they are specialised they may have little attraction for buyers. Current assets are important for liquidity. Cash is the most liquid, then debtors, then inventory.

Figure 10.1: Too little working capital

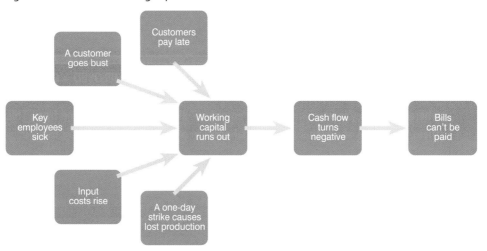

Calculating current ratio and acid test ratio

Two ratios measure liquidity and show how much money there is to pay the bills – the **current ratio** and the **acid test ratio**.

The current ratio measures the ability of a business to meet its short-term debt obligations.

$$\text{Current ratio} = \frac{\textbf{Current assets}}{\textbf{Current liabilities}} \quad \textit{(the answer is expressed as a ratio)}$$

Example

The current ratio of Skiprigg Ltd is $\dfrac{£110,000}{£50,000}$ = 2.2

This means that for every £1 owed by the business, it has £2.20 in current assets with which to pay. This is quite good – as a rough guide the current ratio should typically be between 1.5 and 2.0.

Current ratios may vary according to the type of business and the amount trade fluctuates. However, the current ratio includes inventory which is not always easy to sell. The business also has to keep some inventory to continue trading.

A more reliable measure of liquidity is the acid test ratio, which shows the number of times by which cash and debtors cover short-term liabilities. Inventory is excluded because a business may not be able to convert it into cash quickly enough. This assumes that debtors will pay up. A small firm made to wait for payment by bigger customers has a delay turning debts into cash.

$$\text{Acid test ratio} = \frac{\text{Current assets} - \text{stock}}{\text{Current liabilities}} \qquad \textit{(the answer is expressed as a ratio)}$$

Example

The acid test ratio of Skiprigg Ltd is $\dfrac{£110{,}000 - £60{,}000}{£50{,}000} = 1.0$

With a ratio of 1, the business has exactly £1 available for each £1 of debt. If the ratio was less than 1 e.g. 0.80 it would mean that it only had 80p for each £1 of debt and may be unable to pay its bills. Generally speaking a ratio of 1.0 to 1.2 is good, if it is higher than 1.5 it suggests that the business has too much cash which may be better used elsewhere.

Ways to improve liquidity

The liquidity of a business depends on the ratio of current assets to current liabilities. To improve liquidity current assets need to be increased or current liabilities reduced. In the previous chapter we looked at how a business could increase profitability. Those measures will also help to improve liquidity. Increased profit means increased cash and reduced costs mean lower current liabilities.

A more efficient use of fixed assets can also help improve liquidity; they could be sold off and replaced by leasing to generate cash. Some assets may no longer be needed; for example, a business may own a small building storing seldom used assets, such as older equipment. The equipment could be sold, and then the business could rent out the building to create more revenue and liquidity. A business could raise more capital so current assets are financed by long term sources of finance. Cash required to pay interest on short term borrowing will be reduced, improving liquidity.

Careful management of accounts is vital; debtors are a current asset but cannot be used to pay bills, so invoicing promptly and persuading customers to pay up on time will improve cash flow. Taking maximum advantage of suppliers' credit terms delays payment and keeps cash for other needs. Should a firm have idle cash, it can be put into an interest bearing account until needed. Using external services such as factoring can improve liquidity. Factoring has the debt of a firm collected by a bank or any other financial institution for a fee.

Reducing inventory by turning stocks into cash will improve both the acid test ratio and liquidity. Firms can aim for the minimum stock level needed to run the business efficiently. Then the business should manage stock levels carefully, both of materials and finished goods. Getting output off to customers fast can bring in revenue sooner. Too much inventory ties up cash and worsens liquidity.

Purchasing raw materials or components on a just-in-time (JIT) basis improves cash flow and minimises the money tied up in stock. Storing less stock also reduces the space needed. Computer manufacturer Hewlett Packard introduced just-in-time working into a circuit board plant and reduced the value of the stocks they held from $670,000 to $20,000.

Just-in-time can improve liquidity.

Activity

Simplified balance sheet for Jaguar Land Rover 31st March 2014 (£m)

Total fixed assets	**8,359**
Inventory	2,174
Debtors	2,796
Cash	2,260
Total current assets	**7,230**
Creditors	6,134
Total current liabilities	**6,134**
Net current assets	**1,096**
Assets employed	**9,455**
Long term liabilities	3,591
Share capital	1,501
Reserves	4,363
Capital employed	**9,455**

Give an example of an inventory, an intangible asset, a debtor and a creditor that Jaguar Land Rover might have.

Calculate the current and acid test ratios for Jaguar Land Rover. Comment on your findings.

Suggest ways in which Jaguar Land Rover might be able to improve its liquidity.

The cycle of working capital

We have seen why cash is as important as profit. Working capital management can achieve a balance between having sufficient working capital and liquidity but no excess to reduce profit.

Working capital is current assets minus current liabilities.

The operating cycle (also called the working capital cycle) is the length of time between expenditure (on raw materials, wages and other items) and the inflow of cash from the sale of goods. The operating cycle determines the amount of working capital a business needs. The longer the operating cycle, the more working capital needed.

Figure 10.2: The operating cycle

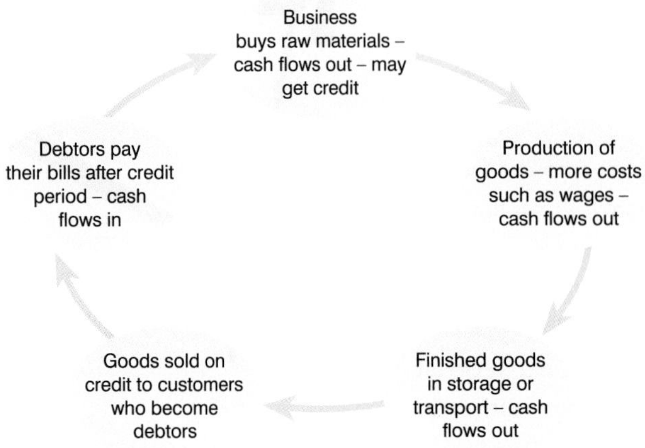

Business buys raw materials – cash flows out – may get credit

Production of goods – more costs such as wages – cash flows out

Finished goods in storage or transport – cash flows out

Goods sold on credit to customers who become debtors

Debtors pay their bills after credit period – cash flows in

The operating cycle shown in Figure 10.2 has time lags; gaps between cash leaving the business and eventually coming back in. A business needs raw materials for production, these could entail credit or cash, either way payment is likely to leave the business before customer revenue appears.

Production turns resources into products, over a time which depends on the product. For builders this could be months for a house to be completed. During this time, further costs need to be paid such as wages, power and overheads. Finished products may spend time in a warehouse before being delivered to customers. Further costs are incurred in storing and delivering the product.

Once goods have finally reached the customer there is another time lag, that of the credit period offered to customers. This can vary between 30 and 90 days. When payment finally arrives it is used to buy more supplies and so the cycle continues.

Managing the operating cycle to reduce time lags reduces working capital needs and improves liquidity. The faster a business can turn around its operating cycle, the more efficiently it will manage its working capital. It can do this by efficient management of inventory, extending its own credit terms with suppliers and speeding up payments from debtors, for example.

Firms have different length operating cycles, therefore different working capital needs. A supermarket chain is in a strong position; their considerable buying power can persuade suppliers to offer keen prices and favourable credit terms. Then goods are usually sold quickly for cash.

Amazon is in a similar position, If it orders 500,000 copies of an eagerly awaited DVD such as 'The Minions', they should pay Universal Studios within 30 days. By the twentieth day, they may have sold all the DVDs and made a profit, before they have to pay. If Amazon can do this with all of its suppliers, it doesn't need much cash on hand to pay its debts. As long as transactions are timed correctly, they will be able to pay each bill as it comes due, maximising their efficiency.

Smaller businesses can face a very different situation, as powerful suppliers may insist on payment with order, particularly for new businesses with no established good credit record. This puts more pressure on working capital.

Many businesses operate in markets with seasonal changes in demand. Cash outflows may be steady throughout the year but cash inflows can be highly seasonal. Firework manufacturers are one example, so are travel agents whose bookings peak in the New Year and farmers who harvest most crops in summer and autumn. Working capital management has to allow for these variations.

Even with careful management, unexpected events can disrupt the working capital cycle, ranging from the mundane to the catastrophic. Road works outside a shop can suddenly decrease revenue, bad weather can mean a poor harvest for farmers, and the 2011 Tohoku earthquake and tsunami in Japan had far reaching impacts on many businesses, including Nissan in the UK and Apple in the US.

Good capital management keeps the cash available to a business ahead of its current payments. Sufficient cash flow to pay employees, debts and liabilities is vital. Reacting promptly and decisively to the competition and to market changes could affect liquidity. An effective working capital management strategy should be able to deal with such things and help the business to succeed.

Demand for fireworks is highly seasonal.

Chapter 11

Business failure

Names from the past

Blockbuster, Woolworths, Phones 4U, Zavvi/Virgin Megastore and Comet were once famous names. They have all now ceased trading and can be counted as business failures.

Questions

1. What do you think caused previously successful businesses like these to fail?
2. Think of a business in your area that has closed – what factors led to its failure?

There are many reasons businesses fail: lack of finance, changes in the economy, ineffective management, changes in demand, more efficient competition and poor marketing are just a few. Some businesses fail completely and cease to exist; others fail with some products but manage to survive as a poorer but wiser firm. It is rarely just one cause that leads to failure; it is more often a combination of issues. Most problems only become apparent when symptoms such as poor sales figures or a loss appear, although the underlying causes may have been at work for some time.

McDonald's is one of the world's most iconic and successful brands, yet has had failures. In 1996 they introduced the 'Arch Deluxe' which never caught on. It was a luxury burger intended to appeal to sophisticated consumers. McDonald's spent $100 million on promotion, making this one of the most expensive product failures in history. Even Apple, currently the world's most successful business has had failures. Its Newton PDA was priced from $700. It was 8 inches tall and 4.5 inches wide, and its handwriting recognition was so bad that a classic Simpsons episode made fun of it. It failed.

Internal and external causes of business failure

Reasons for business failure can be split into two main groupings; internal factors, within the business itself, self-inflicted if you like, and those outside the control of the business and caused by external factors. The internal causes tend to build up unnoticed over time, until they reach a tipping point and can no longer be ignored. This often means lack of cash and a failure to pay bills on time. External causes tend to be more sudden. If the firm is not prepared or lacks sufficient resources, they can have catastrophic results. This point emphasises the importance of contingency planning. Many business blame external causes even when the real failures are internal.

Internal factors: Management vision and strategy

The 2014 Turnaround Management Society (TMS) comprehensive survey of business failures overs five years identified a range of management factors that lead to businesses closures. The percentage figures refer to the frequency with which each was identified as major causes of business failure.

The survey found that mistakes made by the top management were the most common internal causes. They identified a strategy that was no longer working (54.6%), and often losing touch with the market and customers (51.6%). Some businesses had no clear strategy and so made poor choices (39.4%), while others failed to notice changes in the market. If managers follow outdated ideas for too long, whilst the competition is adapting to changing needs in the market, or they underestimate new entrants and/or products, failure is likely.

In a fast changing dynamic market the leadership or vision needed to push a business forward is crucial. Maintaining a competitive advantage by innovation or striving to outdo the competition is important. Businesses without clear leadership tend to drift with no strategic direction and then be outpaced by more energetic rivals. This was identified in 51.4% of business failures.

Lack of internal communication was also a major cause of business failure (33.3%). Management had a tendency not to communicate quickly or efficiently once problems started. When a business is in trouble different departments need to co-ordinate and communicate on plans to remedy the situation. Failure to do so can make matters worse and lead to the failure of the business.

Internal factors: Financial

It is no surprise that liquidity and cash flow are major causes of business failure. Inadequate financial management, poor accounting procedures and lack of financial planning all bring liquidity problems. Maintaining liquidity and careful management of working capital are crucial to the survival of a business. New businesses are particularly susceptible to liquidity problems from overtrading.

> One of the largest bookstores in the United States, Borders, closed in 2011 because of huge debts. It had borrowed over $40 million at high interest rates, and was facing costly repayments. At the same time it was facing very strong competition from both electronic books and online retailers. With falling revenues and high costs the result was inevitable.

Internal factors: Marketing

The product is central to the success or failure of a firm; if a rival comes up with a better one or customers do not like it the business is in trouble. The classic example of this is New Coke, the replacement for the classic Coca-Cola. Customers hated it, after three months the company had to make a U-turn and bring back the original flavour. Lack of investment in future products and technologies means missed opportunities; production methods can become outdated and costly compared to efficient rivals. Products may lack the edge needed, especially in fast moving markets. Businesses that gain a reputation for poor quality and/or poor customer service are in trouble.

Even with a good product, other aspects of marketing can cause problems, too high a price can restrict sales and revenue. Inadequate or inappropriate promotion may give a poor impression of the brand. Brands can also get a bad reputation which is hard to shake off. The ultimate example of this was Gerald Ratner, founder of Ratner's jewellery chain, who said in public that his products were "total crap". Customers voted with their feet. The business lost £500m and was taken over.

Internal factors: Expansion

Expanding into new markets at home or overseas can be fraught with danger; some of the world's most successful businesses have come unstuck here. Tesco tried to enter the lucrative American market with a chain of stores called 'Fresh and Easy', only to withdraw after a £150m loss. Even the mighty Apple is struggling to gain market share in China.

Entering a new market or launching a new product is expensive and the outcome is uncertain. Heavy expenditure is necessary before returns start to come in, taking us back to the problem of liquidity. Distribution and supply networks need to be established and if the new market is overseas there are the added complications from communication, language and cultural barriers and management from a distance. Even a joint venture partner might not help here, as Danone found in 2009 when it sold its share of a joint venture at a 21% loss, following a legal dispute with a Chinese partner.

External factors: Market changes

Markets might not often change much from day to day, but they change considerably over time. Demand for some products and services declines and disappears, whilst others do the opposite. This process of structural change is a natural part of an economy. Unfortunately for some businesses, they get left behind by events, facing falling demand and eventually exiting the market. The armourers of the 16th century, carriage makers at the turn of the 20th century, coal mines in the 1980s, makers of typewriters and of film cameras have all suffered from structural change.

External factors: Competition

A business can get left behind if it doesn't keep up with the competition or changes in a market driven by consumers. Motor World, a car spares and accessories retailer with 34 stores went into administration in March 2015, as a result of strong competition both online and offline. On a much bigger scale, General Motors went bankrupt in 2009 after operating for over a century. The main reason was that it didn't produce vehicles that could compete in a changing global economy.

Businesses that rely too much on a single customer are vulnerable if that customer decides to go elsewhere. Ensemble Clothing, a work wear and clothing retailer in Washington, Tyne & Wear, failed early in 2015. It lost a major contract and suffered severe cash flow problems as a result.

External factors: Financial crisis

The financial crisis of 2008 was the biggest shock to the business world in the last 50 years. The impact is still felt today, finance is still hard to obtain from banks, for example. Many seemingly impregnable businesses such as the world's biggest investment bank, Lehman Brothers, came crashing down; Northern Rock and Bradford & Bingley in the UK suffered the same fate.

The UK and many other Western economies plunged into recession. Businesses lost sales revenue as unemployment rose and consumer confidence fell, this created liquidity problems. At the same time, remaining banks cut lending to help their own liquidity and balance sheets. This left many businesses denied access to extra working capital which could have helped them survive. The XL Leisure Group was a major tour operating company in the UK, which collapsed in late 2008 blaming the economic downturn, high fuel prices and an inability to obtain further funding.

External factors: Economic

Apart from the unique circumstances that created the 2008 crisis, and other shocks, the economy changes over time through the economic cycle. There are recessionary periods when the UK economy shrinks, negative GDP growth causes rising unemployment and many businesses fail. Recessions hit the UK in the early '80s and '90s and there was a slight downturn in the early '00s. Businesses that suffer most in recession tend to have income elastic demand for their products.

Inflation can be damaging, as even in the last recession inflation still rose. The main cause was 'imported inflation'; commodities including food and especially oil were rising in price, pushing up costs for many businesses. Firms already struggling with poor sales and liquidity problems faced extra difficulties and some did not survive, especially those where import costs were a high proportion of their total outgoings.

External factors: Exchange rates

The UK has a floating exchange rate, which means that its value in terms of other currencies changes over time. This can have an impact on businesses that rely on foreign trade. At the time of writing the pound is

Currency movements made Alpari insolvent.

high in value against the Euro; this makes life difficult for UK export businesses as foreign buyers must spend more Euros to buy British goods. Exports orders are down. When the pound is weak, businesses that import suffer, from raw materials cost increases or more expensive finished goods for retail to consumers. Such problems are greater when demand is price elastic.

A study by SunGard Data Systems polled 275 US businesses of various sizes. It found that 59% of those surveyed had seen a loss or gain of more than 5% from currency fluctuations in the previous year. In early 2015, West Ham FC sponsor Alpari, an online foreign exchange dealer, became insolvent and ceased to trade because of the scale of losses suffered by its clients following Switzerland's decision to scrap a currency ceiling against the Euro.

Even firms that do not directly trade abroad can be adversely affected. The combination of a rising oil price and a weak pound pushes energy and fuel costs up, making trading conditions very difficult for businesses with a heavy reliance on oil or fuel.

External factors: Government regulations

Managers and business leaders often complain about excessive government regulations. They usually mean 'red-tape' and bureaucracy, plus rules that restrain business activity. Those who oppose EU membership argue that too many rules and restrictions from Brussels restrict the competitiveness of UK businesses. Many businesses feel frustrated by government regulations but they are not always the direct cause of business failure. Tobacco restrictions hit cigarette makers, but might just have speeded an inevitable decline. A business struggling with liquidity problems could be brought down by 'a final straw' of, say, costly new health and safety regulations.

External factors: Supplier insolvency

A business does not work in isolation; production may depend on supplies of raw materials or components. If the supplying business becomes insolvent and can no longer operate, the receiving business may be in trouble. If it operates a JIT (Just-In-Time) system with minimal amounts of stock, or there is no alternative supplier, problems will quickly be apparent.

When Lithuania's national airline, FlyLAL – Lithuanian Airlines, closed, and flights to Lithuania by foreign airlines stopped, bankruptcies in hotels and restaurants swiftly followed.

External factors: Natural phenomena

Sometimes there is nothing the business can do; a failure is beyond anyone's control. A farmer, for example, is at the mercy of the elements; bad weather can ruin crops or cause a poor harvest. More extreme events such as an earthquake or volcanic eruption can destroy businesses in seconds. Though this is not strictly a natural phenomenon, terrorist action can have a devastating effect on firms. For example, when visitors stay away tourist revenue vanishes.

Causes of business failure

Internal		External	
Financial	**Non-financial**	**Financial**	**Non-financial**
Cash flow/liquidity	Management error	Exchange rate	Structural change
Poor accounting	Wrong strategy	Interest rate	Market change
	Poor marketing	Loans dry up in crisis	Competition
	Poor quality		Economic
	Lack of investment		Govt. regulations
	Communication		Supplier problems
	Failed expansion		Natural phenomena

Exam style question

Night life

The number of bar, public house (pub) and club businesses which went into liquidation rose as the last recession wore on. Consumer confidence remained weak, cutting consumer spending on entertainment. Disposable incomes had fallen for many customers. Uncertainty over job security meant people kept their purse strings tight, according to Anthony Cork of the accountancy firm Wilkins Kennedy. He added that a rise in alcohol duty had eaten into profit margins.

Many pub landlords are tied to tenancy agreements that determine the prices they can charge. Add to this the availability of relatively cheap alcohol in supermarkets, the ban on smoking in bars and pubs, and perhaps it is not surprising that trade fell and insolvencies rose. Although some firms in the industry have recovered since the recession, closures continue at around 30 pubs per week.

Questions

1. What is meant by 'went into liquidation'?   *(2 marks)*

2. What is meant by 'profit margin'?   *(2 marks)*

3. Explain the effect of weak consumer confidence.   *(4 marks)*

4. If a small pub had revenue of £2,000 per week and a 3% gross profit margin, calculate
   its gross profit. Would the pub be likely to survive? Justify your conclusion.   *(4 marks)*

5. Assess likely reasons for the rate of pub closures.   *(8 marks)*

6. Assess two ways in which a pub could improve its profitability.   *(10 marks)*

Chapter 12

Production, productivity and efficiency

Figure 12.1: UK labour productivity index, January 2008 = 100.

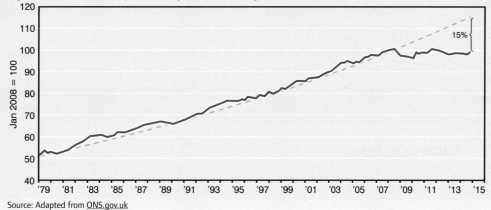

Source: Adapted from ONS.gov.uk

"Weak labour productivity since 2007 has been holding back real wages and well-being. The sustainability of economic expansion, and further progress in living standards, rest on boosting productivity growth, which is a key challenge for the coming years."

Source: OECD Economic Survey of the UK, 2015.

Questions

1. What does this graph show?

2. What would be the benefits of being nearer to the dotted green trend line?

Production is what happens when businesses combine inputs, raw materials and components and process them to produce output of goods and services. This is sometimes called the production process. Production is described either in terms of volume e.g. The UK produced 11.8 billion eggs in 2014 or in financial terms e.g. UK egg production totalled £955 million in 2014.

Productivity describes how effectively productive resources are being used. It is most commonly measured as output per unit of input over a given time period, e.g. how much one worker or machine can produce in an hour, a week or a year. As shown above, UK labour productivity has generally risen over time, but stalled for 6 years from 2008.

Efficiency is a measure of how well production is organised to make best use of resources. Technical or productive efficiency is achieved when the minimum possible inputs are used per unit of output. In other words, production is organised in such a way that costs are the lowest possible and waste of resources is minimised.

Methods of production

Businesses have a choice in how to organise production. This will depend on the nature and quantity of the product being produced. Some products such as bridges or wedding dresses are made to order. Products that are needed in large numbers and standard form will be mass produced on a continuous basis; others that are wanted in smaller numbers may be produced as batches.

Job production

Job production involves the production of a single product at a time. These are 'one-off' jobs and are tailored to suit the requirements of the customer. They can be small in nature such as a made to measure suit, or large such as giant tunnelling machines for the London Crossrail project. Job production often requires a skilled and specialised workforce.

Advantages: Profit margins tend to be high, due to the high value added nature of the work. Output is closely matched to customer needs and can be adapted throughout the production process. Staff are generally motivated by the variety and challenge of the work. Customer relations are close and positive and often personal. Holding little stock as jobs vary cuts costs.

Disadvantages: Labour costs rise for skilled and flexible employees. There is no scope for economies of scale. Capital costs can be high as varied specialist machinery and equipment is needed and may only be used occasionally. Lead times (the time from order to delivery) can be lengthy, and costs may not be recovered until the job is completed, requiring careful management of working capital.

Batch production

Regular demand enables batches to be made together. Manufacturing is split into a number of stages, each of which is carried out on the whole batch until production is complete. Then another batch is started, often with a different specification. Bread production follows more or less the same sequence; mix and knead the ingredients, allow the dough to rise, shape loaves, bake and then cool. E.g. 800g wholemeal loaves, then a batch of 400g white loaves, then a batch of rolls, made in turn.

Advantages: There is still flexibility though quantities are larger; each batch can cater for changing customer tastes and requirements. Some production can be automated and the business can begin to benefit from economies of scale. Capital costs tend to be lower as the production line can be used for different items. Employees need fewer skills, often concentrating on one process, cutting labour costs. New products can be tried, with limited losses if they are not successful.

Disadvantages: Batch production needs careful co-ordination and planning to avoid downtime when workers and machinery are idle. Machines may need to be re-set or cleaned before the next batch. Automated machinery may be complex, increasing start-up costs. The workforce may be less motivated as their task might be repetitive and dull. More stocks of materials and work-in-progress are required, increasing risk and tying up more cash.

Flow production

Flow production has the stages of production carried out in a continuous sequence. This is mass production, used for standardised products on an assembly line. Production is often highly automated and computer controlled. Operations are often carried out by robots (think of car factories in adverts) and jobs tend to be repetitive. Flow production is not always about standard products such as Coca-Cola, many modern automated plants are able to vary specifications to mix colours and trim, for example. This, of course, requires careful co-ordination and planning.

Advantages: Modern flow production is sophisticated, fast and efficient with little of the downtime associated with batch production. High volumes are produced for mass markets, such as food items for supermarkets. Lower unit costs are achieved via economies of scale, particularly as fixed costs are spread over a large output. Skill levels and labour costs can be relatively low.

Disadvantages: Flow production is costly to set up, heavy investment may not earn a return for some time. High demand must continue if a heavy flow is to be maintained. A minor problem or delay can hold up the entire flow. With complex tasks automated, jobs can be repetitive and monotonous, so staff turnover and absenteeism can be high.

Cell production

To remain competitive, businesses need to be able to produce a quality product at minimum cost. Conventional flow production may lead to poor morale and motivation, as outlined above. Newer methods of managing and operating assembly lines aim for the benefits without the disadvantages. Cell production has workers divided into teams which tackle all the stages in production. The team organises itself, decides who does what, organising any training needed and their own breaks. They take responsibility for the quality of output. There are, in effect, lots of 'mini' assembly lines.

Advantages: Team members are multi-skilled, allowing flexible production through job rotation. This and sharing responsibility have a powerful motivating force that increases efficiency. Quality improves because each cell 'owns' its production and cells aim for zero defects and waste. Cell production works well with Just-in-time and requires little stock. At best this can cut costs, improve quality, create a positive reputation and brand image and enhance customer loyalty.

Disadvantages: Cell production has fewer disadvantages than flow production. Some technical economies of scale cannot be reached. Flow production might make use of one complex piece of machinery but it would be wasteful to provide every team/cell with one as it would not be fully used. Management, ordering and stock control can become more complex.

Figure 12.2: Output volume and variety

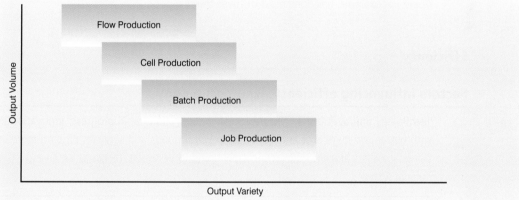

Productivity

 WATCH OUT!

Productivity measures how effectively resources are being used, usually by looking at output per unit of input over a time period. **Production** just measures how much is produced.

Say 10 workers in a factory can make 100 kitchen units a day. The factory then employs another 5 workers and output increases to 150 units per day. Production *has* increased, there is more output but productivity *remains the same* at 10 units per worker per day.

Factors influencing productivity

The amount of capital: Tools and machines enable labour to be more efficient and productive. The more complex they become the more labour productivity increases. Digging a hole in the ground using your hands will take a long time, with a pick and shovel it becomes easier, with a JCB excavator it is physically effortless and very rapid indeed.

Technology: Sophisticated computer systems guide a great deal of production and distribution. Improvements in technology bring improvements in productivity and reduce unit costs.

Human Capital: The skills and abilities of the workforce include general skills from education and also specialist training. Once people are qualified and employed, skills can be developed and updated. Human capital also improves with experience. Skilled and trained workforces produce more. This is one of the differences between more developed and developing countries.

Organising resources more efficiently: If delays cause employees' time to be wasted, productivity suffers. Anything from using available space efficiently to designing complex logistical supply and distribution networks can contribute to productivity.

Link between productivity and competitiveness

Increasing productivity means that more can be produced using the same amount of resources. Another way to look at it is that average cost is being reduced. This brings a firm a competitive advantage. It allows either lower prices and increased sales or constant prices but increased profit margins. Both choices will increase profits. If rivals cannot match your productivity, they will struggle to match your prices and profits.

Having drawn ahead of the competition gives advantages which can keep you in front. Increased profits enable more to be invested back into the business; this can help develop new and better products or improve marketing, which will again improve competitiveness. With higher profits, a firm can also attract the best employees with higher pay, and fund research into yet more productive methods in the future. Apple, for example, has done most of these things.

Efficiency

Factors influencing efficiency: New technology

Technology improves over time and is making ever more rapid progress; innovation provides businesses with better and more efficient ways of producing goods and services. Finding more efficient ways to do things is called process innovation. Downloading Windows 10 could be an example, once users grow familiar with it.

> **Process innovation** means using new technologies to improve production methods, so that costs are reduced.

Better technology brings more efficient capital equipment. It is common for investing in labour-saving equipment and becoming more capital intensive to cut costs of production and increase labour productivity. It may even be possible to raise wage rates and cut prices at the same time. Even labour intensive service industries can improve capital equipment for their workers.

As businesses become more capital intensive, process innovation makes it possible to increase the supply of goods whilst using the same hours of labour (or less). This means productivity increases allowing standards of living to rise. This is an important element in economic growth. It involves change – within the business and for society. Flexible skills become more important. Capital investment is pricey and requires finance for the purchase of new equipment and to fund training to enable people to use the new technologies.

Windows 10 brings process innovation.

Figure 12.3: Gaining from new technology

Factors influencing efficiency: Labour

The human input into the production process is as important as technology. Without skilled, talented and motivated people, full efficiency will not be reached. Capital needs investment to improve it, so too does labour. Ideally, this investment goes beyond full-time education to become an integral part of working life. People learn both new skills and refresh/update existing ones.

Many businesses require multiskilling so that employees can take on different roles as needed; this can motivate the employee and allow the firm to adapt quickly and efficiently. Flexible hours allow some businesses to use labour more efficiently, e.g. with less staff at quiet times. Short-term contracts can bring in specialist skills for a limited time when required.

> **Capital intensive** industries rely heavily on automation and machinery, with a relatively small labour input.
>
> Many service industries are **labour intensive**, relying on human interaction. However, capital can improve efficiency even here. An example is waiters/waitresses sending orders to kitchens via wi-fi.

Factors influencing efficiency: Outsourcing

Shifting all or part of manufacturing and related processes to another specialist provider can improve efficiency. Common examples are accounting and payroll services or plastic mouldings. Because the other business specialises, they are likely to be able to work at a lower average cost and so save money for the original business. When the outsourcing takes place in another country such as China (with cheaper labour) it becomes offshoring. Apple, Sony, Blackberry and other electronic giants use Asian electronics manufacturer 'Foxconn' to make many products and components.

> **Outsourcing** means that a business buys some inputs from other businesses, rather than using its own employees. Outsourcing work to another country is also referred to as **offshoring**.

Factors influencing efficiency: Service industries

Traditionally the service sector has been more labour intensive than manufacturing. It is often less easy to substitute capital for labour in service jobs. Even in the service sector, there are many ways in which efficiency can be improved, with more capital equipment or better organisation.

In areas such as banking, insurance, retailing and tourism, face-to-face contact has been important to customers. High tech developments have reduced the need for so many people to work in the financial sector. The rise of internet retailing has had an impact on high street shops and retail employees. However, areas such as hairdressing, care of the elderly and cleaning remain labour intensive.

The balance between capital and labour

As countries become richer over time, they become able to finance and use more and better capital. The richest and most advanced economies have the most and the best capital equipment. The spectacular growth of the Chinese economy in the last quarter of a century has been based on very rapid accumulation of capital equipment.

This only makes sense with products that are wanted in sufficient quantities to justify the investment. Oil production is particularly capital intensive with oil platforms, pipelines, tankers and so on. Many consumer items are sold in a standard form around the world, so making them in very large quantities and in capital intensive ways become efficient and profitable.

Figure 12.4: Capital and labour

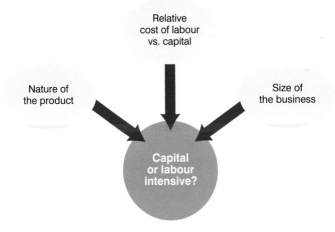

As capital becomes more plentiful it becomes relatively cheap compared to labour. In countries with little capital, it is possible to watch groups of workers struggling with basic equipment to tackle jobs which are quick and easy with advanced equipment. In, say, The Democratic Republic of Congo (DRC), you might find men with crowbars changing car tyres. Their wages are low and there is no money for automated equipment. In the USA specialist machinery takes a couple of minutes to do what can take hours in the DRC.

Although service industries remain relatively labour intensive, extra capital is making inroads there as well. Health care tends to be labour intensive, although it is becoming a little less so as more use is made of capital equipment such as scanners. Doctors are speaking to patients by phone more than in the past. Online 'virtual doctors' are poised to take a growing role.

As firms grow, the use of expensive machinery and equipment becomes more worthwhile and efficient. More capital equipment usually means less labour is needed per unit of output. At one end of the scale, large national jam makers such as Hartley's operate with very sophisticated machinery and large automated production lines, selling to the national market. By contrast, 'Wild and Fruitful', a small business in Wigton, Cumbria, produces jars of jam in a very traditional, labour-intensive way, selling small quantities in their local area where quality products command premium prices. There is a paradox that rich countries can produce cheaply in bulk but many consumers value handmade and distinctive items.

Exam style question

Evaluate the suggestion that all service industries will become increasingly capital intensive.

(20 marks)

Chapter 13

Capacity utilisation

Delays at Accident and Emergency (A&E)

People have to wait at accident and emergency departments when demand for the service is greater than its capacity. In most departments, a 'triage' system is used to select the most urgent cases for rapid treatment. This increases delays for less urgent patients. Attendances and delays are greatest at peak periods, such as 10am to midday on Mondays, when over 4,000 people arrive nationally, on average. Facilities are less crowded very early in the morning, but staffing levels are lowest at such times.

Demand has grown as the ageing UK population contains more elderly people, some of whom are frail and vulnerable. Less obviously, demand has also grown as the availability of rapid treatment in General Practitioner surgeries has diminished in many areas.

The capacity of the system depends on its physical resources and crucially on personnel. Health budgets are limited and there is a shortage of specialist A&E doctors and nurses.

Questions

1. Are long waits in accident and emergency departments unacceptable?

2. What can A&E departments do to cope with heavy demand in peak periods?

3. What might a profit seeking business do if demand exceeded capacity some of the time?

Activity

Think about a business that you are familiar with. This might be a part-time job you have or a family business.

Is it always busy, does it produce as much as it could?

Are there times when resources are not being used?

What could it do to improve the situation?

Capacity utilisation can be seen as a measure of efficiency because it shows how much a business' resources are being used. If all available resources are being used then the business is using all of its capacity and cannot produce any more output; it is said to be at 100% capacity utilisation. It does not matter if it is a car factory with a large output or a small village café, the concept of capacity utilisation applies equally to both businesses.

> **Capacity utilisation** measures what proportion or percentage of the maximum possible output is actually produced.

The formula for capacity utilisation is current output divided by maximum possible output x 100, and is expressed as a percentage.

It can be calculated:

$$\text{Capacity utilisation \%} = \frac{\text{Current output}}{\text{Maximum possible output}} \times 100$$

Implications of under-utilisation of capacity

Capacity utilisation is a problem for business managers and can be tricky to get right. Not enough is a problem because productivity and efficiency will fall. Strangely, 100% capacity utilisation can also be a problem as there is no room for error; attempts to stretch production to the limit can cause breakdowns and bottlenecks which also reduce productivity and efficiency.

Under-utilisation of capacity means that some resources are not being used and production is not as high as it could be. If it is not fully using all of its resources then the unused proportion will be standing idle and creating a cost, either directly or as an opportunity cost. Unused capacity will also increase average costs, this is because the total fixed costs are shared over a lower level of output. As a result the average fixed cost will rise and as they are part of average total cost (AFC + AVC = ATC) then this will increase as well.

The figures below could apply to a small production line:

	100% capacity utilisation **Output = 20,000 per year**	**90% capacity utilisation** **Output = 12,000 per year**
Annual total fixed costs	£180,000	£180,000
Average fixed cost	£9	£10

Activity

Imagine a large body press machine shaping car doors, which has capacity of 10,000 doors per day and fixed costs of £100,000 per day.

What is the average fixed cost of producing 10,000 doors and of 2,000 doors?

An increase in average costs indicates a loss of efficiency and will reduce profit margins if the price remains unchanged. If price increases to maintain profit margins, there may be a subsequent loss of competitive advantage and sales. Under-utilisation can lead to loss of motivation as workers may be bored, become frustrated at the lack of opportunities for extra work or fear losing their jobs because they are producing too little.

Profitability and worker motivation are both likely to be better if the business can find some way of improving capacity utilisation without taking the option of piling up unsold stock. Otherwise, there is likely to be increasing pressure to cut capacity. Imagine, for example, an airline consistently only filling 50% of the seats on its planes. The viability of the route, and perhaps even of the airline, would eventually be questioned. Like other service industries, such as restaurants, the airline's brand could also be damaged if customers noticed low occupancy rates.

> **Under-utilisation of capacity** means using less than the full productive potential of a business. Increased AFC and ATC are likely to result from this.

On the other hand, some under-utilisation can be beneficial. Minor hold-ups to production are easier to cope with if they don't cause pressure and delays in a fully extended system. It gives the business flexibility;

special orders from customers can be accommodated, perhaps even rush orders, creating goodwill and the possibility of future orders. Delivery times are likely to be shorter without the potential delays of full or over-utilisation. Machinery and plant require servicing and repairs during their working life, spare capacity enables this to happen without delaying production.

Implications of over-utilisation of capacity

Over-utilisation arises when a business is trying to produce more than its capital equipment and systems were designed for. This too can result in an increase in average costs as bottlenecks, breakdowns and overcrowding are all likely and can all be expected to reduce efficiency.

It may not be possible to accept extra orders or take on potentially lucrative new customers. Maintenance and servicing of machinery means halting production as everything is being kept busy. People are under pressure and the risk of mistakes and accidents increases. Such a situation can lead to increased stress levels for workers and management. This is a variation on the situation of A & E departments at busy times. As with under-utilisation, this means that the business is not as efficient as it could be, average total costs are not minimised.

> **Over-utilisation of capacity** means operating at above the sustainable and lowest cost level of output.

Clearly, both under and over utilisation of capacity have their drawbacks. In an ideal world a business would like to operate with 100% capacity utilisation but in reality this will bring problems and be difficult to sustain. A level of around 90% is probably ideal in many circumstances. This makes good use of most of the capacity but allows for unexpected orders or increases in demand. In individual situations the best balance might sometimes be found at a little more or a little less than 90%.

The more flexible a business can be, the better it will cope with capacity utilisation. Using some part-time or temporary staff and equipment (e.g. hiring extra vehicles or specialist machinery) can make it easier to adjust production and to address bottlenecks. This can keeps labour productivity high and avoid having idle equipment or people with time on their hands, so keeping costs of production to a minimum.

Ways of improving capacity under-utilisation

The simplest response to under-utilisation is just to increase output, producing more to use the spare capacity that exists. However, there is no point in doing this if there is no demand for the extra production, it will just accumulate as unsold stock and may cause cash flow problems. Promotion may be a possible strategy to increase demand, as long as the other aspects of the marketing mix are in place. If the reason for under-utilisation is falling demand due to uncompetitive products then promotion is unlikely to work.

It may be possible to extend the product range with a new product or even to find a new market for the existing one(s). In a global economy, a new export market can often be possible. In 2009 the Jaguar Land Rover (JLR) plant at Halewood was running well under capacity, so much so that there was a three-week shut-down in the autumn and a number of job losses. Things have since changed markedly for the better. JLR introduced a new model, the Range Rover Evoque. Global demand for this luxury SUV has been such that 24-hour operations at Halewood were introduced for the first time in the plant's history. From 2013 the plant was operating at full capacity, something which had not been seen in the previous 50 years.

Taking the same approach further, plants can sometimes be modified to allow entry to a new market where demand is healthier. For example, some shipyards which had become uncompetitive have successfully switched to production of oil and gas exploration and production platforms. The Hadrian's Yard shipyard in Newcastle found a new life in this way.

Sometimes it is possible to use the extra capacity to produce for other businesses rather than the producer trying to sell more. Many food processors have brands of their own and also produce supermarket own label alternatives as a way of utilising spare capacity. Haulage and coach companies often rent out unused vehicles to other businesses that have excess demand.

Persistent under-utilisation can be solved by reducing the resources employed and adjusting the capacity, making changes to supply rather than demand. Assets such as machinery can be sold off or simply scrapped if they have no residual value. Property and land can be sold for alternative uses. A large organisation might be able to transfer surplus labour to other work, otherwise redundancies might be necessary. Once capacity is lost in these ways, it becomes much more difficult to increase production in the future should demand increase. Businesses are reluctant to do this unless they accept that there is a long-term fall in demand for the product.

Ways of improving over-utilisation of capacity

Over-utilisation rarely affects all parts of a business in the same way. What tends to happen is that bottlenecks and shortages appear in some areas. It may be possible to identify and tackle those problem areas; perhaps by minor changes to capital equipment or by diverting labour from a relatively underused area of production to the area that is causing the problems. Where such steps as these are not available in the short run it can be necessary to have waiting lists for customers, to refuse additional orders, or even to increase prices as a way of limiting demand.

Examining the way production is organised and performed can uncover ways that efficiency and output levels can be improved. This applies not just to production systems, but also to management and supply systems as well. Lean production is aimed at improving all areas of the business to yield maximum efficiency. Rationalisation is an umbrella term for reorganising production in a more logical, coherent and efficient way.

Another possibility is to increase working hours. Thornton's Chocolate operates 24 hours a day with three eight hour shifts in the build up to Valentine's Day. This enables the business to produce more without further investment in capital equipment. On a smaller scale, working overtime can be a simpler way to

Thornton's Chocolate operates 24 hours a day in the build up to Valentine's Day.

increase production. Alternatively, It may be possible to outsource or sub-contract some production or processes to other businesses, either on a temporary basis or a permanent one if demand remains high.

The best long term solution is to invest in increased capacity. JLR was running at full capacity by 2013 and has invested more than £230 million in the plant to create new and bigger production facilities. £45m of that went on a new press machine over 13 metres tall and over 85 metres long which reduces the time it takes to change die casts (moulds made from metal), from 55 minutes to 5 minutes. This will add hours of extra production per week. Increasing capacity is a costly process and should only be considered when the business is confident that the extra demand will continue for the medium and long term. JLR obviously thinks it is, and is making these investments based on rising global demand in the overseas markets it supplies, particularly in China.

Investment in new plant and capacity often offers access to new and improved technology. One long term trend is for production to become more capital intensive. Production tends to become less labour-intensive as automation, for example, reduces the labour requirement per item produced. This contributes to long term improvements in labour productivity and in the productive potential of the whole economy.

Improving under-utilisation	• Promotion • New products/markets • Produce for other businesses • Sell unused assets

Improving over-utilisation	• Rationalisation • Extra labour • Outsource • Investment

Activity

In 2012 69,300 motorcycles were produced in the UK, when the estimated potential capacity was 82,500. Industry operating profit margins fell from an estimated 12.5% to approximately 6.0% in 2012-13.

Calculate the capacity utilisation of the UK motorcycle industry in 2012-13.

Explain the link between under-utilisation of capacity and profitability.

Assess two possible approaches that UK motorcycle manufacturers could take to improving their capacity utilisation.

Chapter 14

Stock control

John Deere

Bob Lane took charge of the American agricultural-equipment firm John Deere in 2000. He found old and slow working practices. There was too much working capital and too much stock sitting unsold in showrooms. It was, said Bob Lane, "asset-heavy and margin-lean".

He introduced lean production with the Deere Production System (DPS), which is adapted to its unique needs. "We are not an automobile company with huge volumes," Lane says. "What you have is lots of different products – planters, sprayers, combines, tractors – all of them quite different. So our Deere Production System is tailored to low-volume, high-quality production." Productivity increased by 11% and the share price rose by over 300%.

By 2012 problems had appeared, farmers complained of long waiting times for equipment and some started to buy from rival manufacturers. John Deere had focused on becoming a build-to-order company, reducing stock to a minimum. That increased profitability by reducing the amount of materials and working capital the company needed. This worked well when demand was steady or falling, as it was in the recession, but when demand picked up production began to lag behind and shortages occurred.

Questions

1. Why might (a) too much working capital and (b) too much stock have been a problem?

2. What do you understand by the phrase "asset-heavy and margin-lean"?

3. Consider options open to John Deere to restore sales and profitability.

> **Stock** is a term used to cover everything from raw materials through work-in-progress to fully finished products that the business is holding.
>
> **Stock control** is the process of making sure that the optimum level of stock is held so that demand can be met while keeping the costs of holding that stock to a minimum.

Interpretation of stock control diagram

The classic stock control model assumes that stock is used at a fairly constant rate and can be shown as a chart.

Figure 14.1: Stock control chart

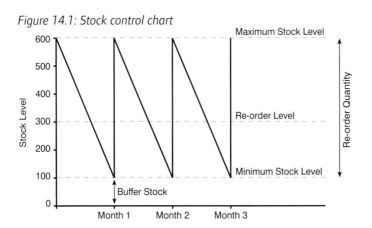

The stock control model is read from left to right. As production takes place stock is used up and the level of remaining stock decreases. This is being monitored and more supplies are ordered when it reaches a level known as the re-order level. There will be a time-lag between ordering new stock and the supplier delivering it. In the meantime production continues and the stock level continues to fall. If all goes well, new supplies arrive as the minimum stock level is reached and stock levels are replenished, then the pattern repeats itself.

Buffer stocks

In an ideal world the business would run out of stock precisely when new supplies arrive, but this is risky. A delay with the delivery may halt production so a business keeps a small supply of emergency stock in case of this eventuality. This is called a buffer stock. McDonald's uses a system like this; their restaurants hold a small buffer stock. This is an extra quantity of stock held to meet delayed delivery or unexpectedly higher demand. Dipping into this extra stock acts as a signal to order more supplies.

Implications of poor stock control

Stock control can be a problem for business managers...

Too much stock	• Increased costs • Cash flow problems may result

Too little stock	• Production may be halted • Cannot meet orders and so lose customers

Efficient stock control allows a business to have the stock it needs, in the right place at the right time. This ensures that capital is not tied up unnecessarily but also protects production if problems arise in the supply chain (the various suppliers that contribute inputs to the production process).

Too much stock can be a problem for two main reasons. Firstly, it has to be stored somewhere; this means using space with both a direct cost and an opportunity cost. It is expensive to store stock, it requires labour and equipment to handle it and move it around the place, and the storage space might otherwise be used for extra production. Perishable stock deteriorates over time, for example McDonald's salad ingredients would become waste if stored for too long.

Secondly, cash is tied up in the stock and cannot be used elsewhere; this can then lead to cash flow problems. Even if this does not cause liquidity problems there is the opportunity cost, since cash tied up in stock cannot be used elsewhere in the business to create further growth and profitability.

Too little stock brings the obvious risk of running out at a crucial time, with production forced to grind to a halt. Fixed costs still need to

Too much stock can be a problem.

be paid and there is also the value of the lost output and revenue to be taken into account. Lack of production may lead to disappointed customers who may become reluctant to place further orders.

Just-in-time (JIT) management of stock

> **Just-in-time** (**JIT**) is a stock control system that does away with the need to hold large quantities of stocks or raw materials. Stocks arrive as and when they are needed – hence the name.

JIT is a system of production that keeps stock levels to a minimum. Rather than having large amounts of stock which is inefficient, JIT relies on frequent deliveries of small quantities of supplies as and when they are needed. This involves close relationships between the suppliers and the producer, to ensure that supplies do actually arrive in time and that the quality of components is totally reliable. It may be necessary to install sophisticated computerised stock control systems to ensure this level of co-ordination and ensure that stocks never actually run out. This removes the need to hold large reserve stocks which are expensive to purchase and store.

JIT has some clear advantages; holding less stock saves on costs and improves liquidity. Space that might have been needed for stock is freed up and can be used for production. It becomes easier for the business to be flexible and respond to special orders or to changes in demand. A minor drawback is that only buying in small amounts of supplies at a time could remove savings from cheaper bulk purchases. However, this is amply compensated for by the advantages of using JIT.

JIT has one major potential problem, the business depends on the supplier, late deliveries or a poor quality batch of components can disrupt production and be costly. This is why a good relationship with suppliers is so important. Before Toyota will accept a new supplier they will send in teams to check out their operational and logistical systems. If these are not good enough Toyota will send in teams to change them to get the reliability and quality they want. This creates a lean supply system where close co-operation and working together with a sole supplier is seen as much more efficient than sourcing from several different suppliers who are all competing on price.

> **Lean supply** refers to the idea of eliminating waste in the supply chain by a process of collaboration and co-operation.

Keeping buffer stocks is expensive. A just-in-time system of stock control can avoid this.

With a JIT system, the stock control chart looks different because the buffer stock is eliminated, part of the cost of storing stocks is saved.

Figure 14.2: Just-in-time stock control

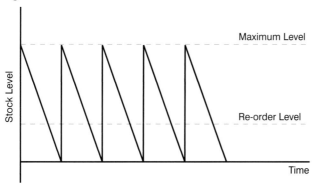

Nike

Nike, one of the world's biggest manu-facturers of sports and leisure clothing, operates a lean supply system. A contract manufacturer has to undertake a process called 'Factory sourcing' to be accepted by Nike as a supplier. Nike spends time, money and resources helping the potential supplier reach Nike's exacting standards. This process takes on average 152 days.

What is a lean supply system?

Explain why Nike devotes so much time and money to helping its suppliers.

Explain any possible disadvantages to a lean supply system.

Waste minimisation

Henry Ford, a man ahead of his time in many ways, had much to say on waste. In his book 'My Life and Work', he described a farmer carrying water up a ladder rather than spending money to install water pipes as 'waste motion', and argued that spending on improvements was not wasted money at all but an increase in efficiency.

Reducing waste is a key idea behind much of lean production (see next section) and modern business operations. It has a wider meaning than just reducing rubbish or producing fewer faulty products. It is an all-encompassing idea that tries to get as much output as possible out of the smallest amount of inputs by examining every stage of production to try to make efficiency gains.

The Japanese word for waste in a business – *Muda* – means any activity or process that wastes time or resources or fails to add any value so ultimately reduces profitability. The production process consumes resources and waste occurs when more resources are used than are essential to produce the goods and services the market wants. In other words, Muda is about increasing productivity and efficiency by trimming out unnecessary actions that just add to costs rather than profit.

Muda has evolved to identify the following areas where waste can be minimised:

Areas where waste can be minimised

Transport	Unnecessary movement of stock or product between operations and/or locations
Stock	Optimising the level of stock held
Motion	Unnecessary movement of people or machinery during their work
Waiting	People and machinery should not be waiting for other production stages to finish
Over-production	Producing products or services beyond the customer's requirements
Defects	Output that is damaged or not fit to be sold
Talent	Not recognising and making full use of the talents of the workforce
Resources	Wasting power and energy
By-products	Not making full use of any by-products from the production process

Minimising waste in all areas of a business involves examining production or operational systems to see if they can be improved. If supplies arrive and are unloaded and stored in a warehouse a long way from the production line, it will take time to transport them to where they are needed. This is waste; could those supplies be stored any closer to where they are used? A worker has to cross from one machine to another to complete an assembly process, could the machines be put next to each other? A light left on or heating that is set too high are both waste, could they be turned off or turned down? A worker who is waiting for the forklift truck to deliver a batch of components, why the delay?

These may seem like small steps but they add up and increase the efficiency of the business. For example, one small part of Nike's lean production programme is a target to reduce the weight of its shoe boxes by 10% over the next four years, thus reducing packaging costs. We have looked at the importance of stock control and JIT; later sections will look at other aspects of production such as quality. These areas are also crucial to waste minimisation.

Competitive advantage from lean production

Figure 14.3: The key areas of lean production

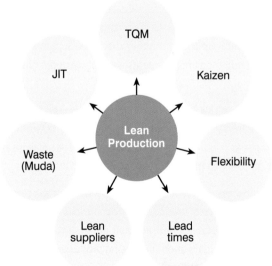

'Lean and mean' is an oft-used expression conveying the idea that a business that is lean is also strong and very competitive.

> **Lean production** is a general term given to any system of production that tries to minimise waste during the production process. This helps to cut costs.

Right up to the 1980s, managers in the West usually felt that quality and reliability depended on a rigid approach to business management. Strict rules were dictated by top managers for employees to follow. However, Japanese manufactured products had become famous for their reliability and quality of design. This had been achieved using lean production methods and a very different management style – sometimes called the 'Japanese Way'.

Ideas behind lean production have been around for a long time. Some Japanese manufacturers, in particular Toyota, systematically studied and developed the approach. In the 1950s, Toyota began looking for strategies which would increase productivity and cope with a general scarcity of resources in post-war Japan. This drove Toyota to change conventional, mass-production manufacturing to produce a wider range of models in smaller quantities. Toyota changed from a 'push' (build and then sell), to a 'pull' (sell and then build) method of production. This enabled them to eliminate waste across the system (e.g. over-production, too much stock, poor quality).

Out of this came lean production, which combines components including:

- JIT – Just-in-time
- Time-based management
- TQM – Total Quality Management
- Kaizen – continuous improvement
- Waste minimisation
- Flexibility – in all aspects
- Short lead times
- Lean supply chain

Lean production's more flexible approach sought continuous improvement as well as waste elimination. This called for every employee to be part of a team seeking better ways of organising production and making better products. It required excellent communication at every level of the business. Gradually, aspects of lean production were widely adopted in Western economies.

TQM and Kaizen focus on the importance of quality and the need for continuous improvement. Some businesses find these approaches fit well with democratic leadership, which encourages individuals to collaborate, sharing ideas and using team work to develop new products or procedures (see the next section).

Lean and flexible production allows businesses to adapt to dynamic markets and changing circumstances more quickly, and to offer customers what they want in a short period of time. Lean production reduces product development lead times; the shorter this time is, the faster the new product can get to market. Businesses that can quickly and efficiently respond to new orders will get more customers and a competitive advantage.

> **Product development lead time** starts from the first idea about the product, through the design and development period, to being ready to start selling the finished product.

Short lead times reduce costs. Development of products is expensive; cash is spent with no incoming sales revenue. The less time spent on this, the lower the cost and the sooner the product reaches the customer and sales revenue begins to flow. A short lead time will reduce the development stage of the product life cycle from Theme 1. In addition there is the advantage of getting the product to market before competitors, sometimes called 'first mover advantage'. This is another source of competitive advantage.

Five years ago it took Intel, the world's largest computer chip maker, 14 weeks to produce a new chip. Today they take just 5 days using lean principles.

Greater flexibility in the use of both capital and labour makes short production runs possible. Where capital equipment can be used to produce a range of differentiated products, the business will be able to adapt easily to market changes. Similarly, if labour is multi-skilled and willing to switch jobs when necessary, adaptability will be greater. Short production runs mean that the business can cut production as soon as a downturn in demand is seen, so few products will fail to sell. Flexible capital equipment, labour and management are essential to redesign a product quickly in response to market forces.

> **Time based management** is based on saving time wherever possible. For many businesses, the speed with which they can respond to change is a key factor in maintaining competitiveness. It requires flexibility in all aspects of the business.

Lean production was developed in the manufacturing sector but it can be applied to services as well. Obviously, JIT is most likely to be found in factory-based manufacturing, but the communications, motivational and organisational aspects of lean production can be applied in almost any working environment. The use made of each aspect of lean production will depend on the context and much depends on the corporate culture of the business. A major European bank used lean techniques to reduce processing time for mortgage applications to 5 days, from 35. Fewer applicants dropped out of the process, so the bank's revenues grew by 5% even as processing costs fell by 35%.

Lean Production: a summary

Advantages of lean production	Disadvantages of lean production
• Reduces wastage and related costs.	• Does not suit all production processes.
• Reduces costs of storage and handling.	• Failure by one small supplier can halt the entire production process.
• Improves quality.	• Workers may dislike greater responsibility.
• Lower costs from fewer rejects.	• Managers and staff may not be flexible enough.
• Customers more satisfied with quality.	
• Greater flexibility.	
• Shorter lead times.	
• More motivated staff, less staff turnover.	

Quality management

Quality control

Quality control refers to the traditional methods of checking that products are of a good enough standard, capable of doing what they are intended to do.

Under traditional quality control, inspection of products takes place during and at the end of the operations process. This is usually done by a quality control inspector who will check the product for faults. There is an underlying assumption that errors and defects are an inevitable part of production and that it is the purpose of quality control to check other people's work, find mistakes and put them right. For some products, there might be sample inspections, or a target may be set, requiring a minimum percentage of the output to be without defects.

This approach can be useful for manufacturing businesses that rely on unskilled or temporary staff. There are however several drawbacks. The system makes no attempt to find out why mistakes happen, as its purpose is simply to prevent faulty goods reaching the customer. It does not find every faulty product; this can mean dissatisfied customers and a costly returns and replacement process as well as a loss of reputation. The whole process reinforces the idea that mistakes are unavoidable and that the workforce do not need to worry about quality as it is someone else's job to find the mistakes. It is expensive in terms of implementation and wastage of stock and does not add value.

Quality assurance

Quality assurance works on a completely different assumption to quality control. It assumes that mistakes can be prevented and that it is possible to produce high quality output all of the time. It involves much more than just an inspection of the end product. It seeks to improve quality throughout production processes as well as in the products and services themselves.

> **Quality assurance** takes into account customer's needs and entails employee involvement in looking at every aspect of the business, sharing in efforts to improve the quality of the product or service.

Quality assurance assumes that mistakes can be prevented.

Quality assurance implies a commitment to collaboration between everyone working in design, production and marketing. It involves working together towards improving quality and reliability at each stage in the production process. Everyone has to become conscious of the need for quality.

This means focusing on prevention of defects, rather than just checking for any that have already happened. Some businesses have a zero-defects policy, which means getting the product right first time so that wastage is minimised, reducing costs as a consequence.

Successful quality assurance comes through various approaches. It may mean changing the corporate culture of the business, so that all employees see quality as a high priority that influences all aspects of their work. A corporate culture that takes quality issues seriously will help to ensure that all employees feel involved and committed to maintaining quality in both the product and the production process. Systems are developed to deliver high standards at each stage of production. These could use the international standard ISO 9000, or codes of practice that have been developed for the industry concerned, as well as each firm's unique ideas.

> **ISO 9000** is a series of standards, developed and published by the International Organization for Standardization (ISO), that define, establish, and maintain an effective quality assurance system for manufacturing and service industries.

Benchmarking involves comparing your business performance with other businesses that have excellent quality standards. The objectives of benchmarking are to see how other businesses reach their high standards, to determine where improvements might be needed, and then use this information to improve performance.

It also involves techniques and strategies discussed elsewhere in this book such as kaizen, quality circles and total quality management (TQM). Quality assurance strategies are an important element in the implementation of lean management. Many businesses will expect their own quality assurance standards to be applied in supplier businesses as well.

Quality circles

Quality circles are small groups of employees that meet regularly to look at how quality can be improved. Any recommendations are passed to management for possible implementation.

Quality circles meet up and discuss issues to do with quality, either in general terms or to specifically to analyse a problem and to solve it. They include representatives from different departments in the organisation and from different levels in the hierarchy. They can be very effective as they bring together the people with knowledge and experience of production, such as the shop floor workers, and the people with the ability to implement new ideas, such as senior management.

Besides improving and maintaining quality standards, quality circles have the added advantage of involving and empowering staff, which is likely to improve their motivation. In turn, this may lead to an improvement in productivity as well as quality. However, they only work if management fully support and participate in the process, listen to suggestions that are made and then act on them. It is important that involvement should be voluntary; staff who feel obliged or pressured to join in are less likely to make useful or relevant contributions. A common problem arises from managers setting up circles for which they appoint themselves as leaders; this stifles creative discussion and maintains the established hierarchy, which quality circles are supposed to break out of.

Toyota has been engaged in quality circles since the early 1960's as part of their TQM programme. After 50 years of making improvements by this method Toyota has reached the stage where a 0.05% defect level in machining is deemed 'problematic' and needs working on.

Total Quality Management (TQM)

Total Quality Management (**TQM**) – all employees are involved in quality control and take responsibility for the quality of their own and their team's work. This helps reduce costly wastage and also reinforces employee motivation.

TQM includes management, employees, design, production, sales and marketing departments. Everyone is committed to improving quality. Each department focuses on the needs of the next department in line and so strives to improve the quality of their stage of production in order to satisfy them. This means that the drive towards quality and reliability runs right through the whole production process.

For TQM to work properly it needs committed leadership, as management must be wholeheartedly behind the scheme. As with other aspects of quality and lean production, employees need a degree of empowerment; they must have greater involvement in their work and greater responsibility to make changes. This requires a training process, as it takes time and effort to make employees aware of their changing role and to appreciate the importance of TQM. The business will need close relationships with customers to meet their needs, and with suppliers to raise the quality of inputs.

Properly implemented TQM should lead to a range of benefits for the business, including a competitive advantage. The quality of its products or services should improve, leading to increased customer satisfaction, repeat purchases and greater brand loyalty. Profitability should improve as costs are reduced and productivity improves from a more motivated workforce.

The down side is that TQM can be a time consuming and costly system to set up and there may be resistance from people in both management and production, who may fear change. The new systems and training needed will inevitably cause some disruption and be expensive, and it may not prove effective for all businesses. Yet the potential benefits are considerable.

Vista Optics ltd. manufactures medical device polymers for applications such as contact lenses. Keen to improve, they adopted the principles of TQM. Rejects on some products fell from 12.4% to 0.2%, delivery performance improved from 90% same day delivery to 99.2%, and profitability rose. A benchmarking exercise saw significant improvements to cash flow and supplier relationships.

Continuous improvement (Kaizen)

Kaizen is the Japanese term for continuous improvement. It summarises a whole company approach to quality control. Kaizen focuses on numerous small improvements rather than sudden or radical change. It is about gradual evolution rather than sudden revolution, seeing more benefits and sustainability in making small improvements to 100 things rather than improving one thing by 100% when problems occur. The key word in kaizen is 'every' because it involves everyone in everything.

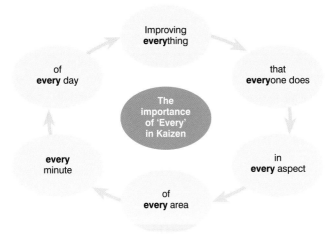

Everyone in the business is involved in the search for improvements to both the product and the process of production. They each take it upon themselves to monitor and improve quality wherever possible. Individual improvements are small and may seem trivial, but they are spread throughout the business. They add up to a continually improving product or service. Customers benefit from a better quality product. Quality circles are just one aspect of this process.

5 Whys

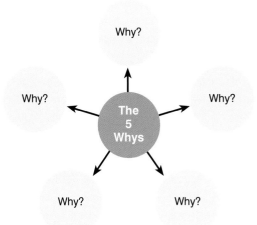

The 5 Whys is a question asking technique that reaches the fundamental causes of a problem. The answer to each question forms the basis of the next question, until the root cause is reached. First developed by Toyota, this forms an integral part of Kaizen and lean production.

5 Whys Example – A customer complains about the late delivery of her order

● Why was the delivery late? – Because production was slow.

● Why was production slow? – Because a machine broke down.

● Why did the machine break down? – Because the bearings seized.

● Why did the bearings seize? – Because they were not maintained properly.

● Why were they not maintained properly? – Because of maintenance staff shortages.

Now the root cause of the problem has been identified and can be tackled.

Kaizen is only effective when everyone participates and the management is wholeheartedly in support. Staff at all levels are given some control over decision making, with a degree of empowerment, appropriate training and access to detailed information about the company. This encourages commitment and interest, leading to job satisfaction, motivation and an increase in productivity.

> First Trans Pennine Express (FTPE) won the 2014 UK Excellence Award. FTPE focused on continuous improvement as part of the delivery of high quality service to customers, improving both the quality of their services and their customer satisfaction rating. Judges praised their leadership programme across the organisation, so that people were empowered, engaged and committed to the organisation's continued success.

Competitive advantage from quality management

In a competitive market quality can be an important source of competitive advantage, enhancing brand image. Consumers may prefer to buy a product that is perceived to be differentiated by better quality than rival products. Better quality not only encourages sales but also leads to customer loyalty and a good reputation. Where a strong reputation for quality means that a premium price can be charged, businesses can gain from increased profit margins. Another aspect to this is that improved quality means less wastage and therefore reduced costs, which again improves profitability. Every defective product has cost the same to produce as a good one but cannot be sold to raise revenue.

Most customers will understand that better quality often entails paying a higher price. They will see a trade-off between price and quality in the range of products available to them. In fact, quality assurance, TQM and continuous improvement may all help to give a competitive edge and to add value in ways that enhance the reputation and performance of a business.

Exam style question (Section C)

Team Sky
Sir Dave Brailsford, general manager of the Sky cycling team and one of the most successful coaches in any sport, speaks about something he calls 'The Aggregation of Marginal Gains'. This means breaking down a process into its constituent parts and building in improvements everywhere, even if the improvement makes that part just 1% better. His belief is that if you improve every area related to cycling by just 1%, those small gains add up to a considerable competitive advantage.

Team Sky searched for marginal gains in tiny areas that were overlooked by almost everyone else: such as finding the pillow that offered the best sleep for riders and taking it with them to hotels, testing for the most effective massage gel, finding a new bike paint supplier to make the coating of paint thinner and lighter, and teaching riders the best way to wash their hands to avoid infection.

Brailsford believed that if Team Sky followed this strategy, they would be in a position to win the Tour de France in five years. He was wrong, it just took three years and Team Sky cyclists have now won three out of the last four Tours.

Question
Evaluate the relevance of TQM and Kaizen to Sir Dave Brailsford's 'Aggregation of Marginal gains'. *(20 marks)*

Chapter 16

Economic influences

Dilmah Tea

A hilly region of southern Sri Lanka has ideal conditions for tea plantations. After 25 years of growth, Dilmah employs more than 30,000 people and exports tea to more than 100 countries.

Sri Lanka has an emerging economy with 20 million people and annual income of £2,300 per capita and rising. Inflation has fallen in 2015 to around 2%. The Sri Lankan exchange rate has fallen a little, with £1 worth SLR220 (Sri Lankan Rupees). Recorded unemployment has risen slightly, to 4.7%. A new government has made changes in 2015, shifting some taxation from households to businesses and cutting back on some big infrastructure projects.

Questions

1. Which of the national economic indicators given for Sri Lanka will have an impact on Dilmah?

2. How might the shift in taxation affect Dilmah's continuing growth?

Within their own business, owners or managers have control of decisions and can make changes when necessary. Outside the business there are economic variables that owners or managers cannot control, which can have a big impact on the situation the firm faces. Governments can take action which affects these variables. However, even governments don't have complete control; millions of people ('economic agents' in this context) make decisions independently. In a globalised economy, there are billions of decision makers influencing world markets.

Inflation

Inflation is measured by index numbers which estimate the overall impact of price changes. In the UK the Consumer Price Index (CPI) is the most used index. For some purposes the older Retail Price Index is still used. Price changes are measured each month; we mainly use an annual figure based on what has happened to prices in the last 12 months.

> **Inflation** is a general rise in the level of prices, measured by an index number such as the CPI. Negative inflation, or deflation, means a fall in the general level of prices and is rarer.

WATCH OUT!

When inflation falls, say from 4% to 2%, prices are still rising. There is only deflation with a minus figure.

Businesses are affected both by the prices of their inputs and by the sale price of their products. When the cost of inputs rises, firms must pay more or make do with fewer inputs. This will not matter very much if all costs and output prices rise by the same amount, but that would be unusual. The ability of firms to put their prices up depends on the actions of rivals (who probably face similar cost changes) and the response of consumers to a price increase (PED). Many firms have debts from borrowing money; inflation reduces the real value of debt, especially high rates of inflation.

Sometimes inflationary pressure comes from growth in demand (called demand-pull inflation). High demand makes it easier for many firms to raise prices, so profits might go up at such times. When cost-push inflation is driven by input prices, the situation is trickier. At such a time, having products with price inelastic demand is very useful as price rises have less impact on quantity sold.

Inflation reduces the spending power of employee earnings; they will want wage increases (a cost to the firm) to protect their standard of living. Many industries and individual businesses have annual wage negotiation rounds. These become more difficult when high inflation is current or expected. This means that even demand-pull inflation is likely to have an impact on firms' costs eventually.

World oil and commodity prices, together with currency appreciation (below), contributed to -0.1% deflation in the year to April 2015, and a four month period with no overall change in prices. Both of these things were unusual for the UK. A concern with deflation is that the expectation of falling prices could lead consumers to delay spending, so demand for businesses could fall. Japan has experience of this but elsewhere it is exceptional.

The target rate of inflation in the UK is 2%. Moderate inflation such as this is relatively easy to live with. Volatility in the inflation rate brings uncertainty – more on this later – which firms dislike. Rapid inflation brings 'menu costs' from frequently revising prices and costings. The worst case scenario is hyperinflation, when prices rise so quickly that money ceases to function effectively and many businesses struggle to survive.

Exchange rates

UK businesses depend on overseas suppliers for many of their inputs and overseas customers for a good proportion of their sales. Overseas suppliers want payment for our imports in their own currencies, so the exchange rate will influence the £sterling price for UK buyers. Similarly, a change in exchange rates will alter the amount foreigners pay for imports from the UK. As most major economies now have '**floating**' exchange rates set by market forces, relative prices change frequently and this is another area where businesses can face uncertainty.

The graph below shows an index value of sterling against a 'basket' of other currencies.

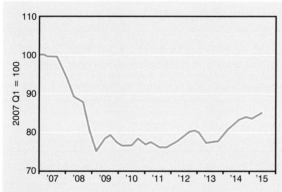

Figure 16.1: The value of sterling

Source: OBR

Sterling lost 25% of its value between 2007 and 2009. If £1 had started that period worth $1.60, this could have fallen to $1.20 by the end. Such **depreciation** could help exporters as the foreign currency price of UK products would fall. Rolls Royce aero engines priced at £1m = $1.6m in 2007 might sell for £1m = $1.2m in 2009, making them much more competitive for US plane makers. Even in UK markets where home producers compete with imports, dearer import prices should help UK firms. Conversely, depreciation brings greater expense for firms buying imported materials as they face higher costs. The situation gets more complicated if we accept that Rolls Royce, for example, imports materials as well as selling engines, so their UK price could rise, but only some of their inputs will be imported.

The simple truth is that home firms gain from depreciation when selling abroad and lose from depreciation when buying from abroad.

The situation is reversed for **appreciation**, when the value of sterling goes up. As Figure 16.1 shows, the index climbed back up from 75 to round 85 by mid-2015. This means exports getting dearer and so less competitive, but imports getting cheaper. Imports have grown faster than exports in recent months, and UK firms competing with imports have struggled. This time firms buying from abroad gain from lower prices, but export prices rise in other currencies. The effect of this depends on PED.

> A **floating** currency has its value set by market forces of demand and supply, so can fluctuate.
>
> **Depreciation** is the name for a fall in the value of a currency against others.
>
> When a currency rises in value against others, this is an **appreciation**.

Interest rates

Rates of interest vary according to the level of risk, the time period and other factors. However, the initial guidance for rates comes from the **Bank of England base rate**. This was reduced to 0.5% in March 2009, in an attempt to stimulate borrowing and activity during the recession. More than six years later base rate has not changed and loans are still relatively cheap.

> ### Find out
> What is the Bank of England base rate whilst you are studying this section?
>
> If it has risen from 0.5%, why might that change have been made?

A low **interest rate** has three advantages for businesses:

● Any bank loans or overdrafts they take are likely to be relatively cheap, reducing a cost.

● Consumers can borrow cheaply to fund expensive purchases, so demand might rise, e.g. for cars.

● Lower mortgage interest gives many households more spending power so consumption might rise.

Higher interest rates can have the opposite effects so are generally seen as against the interests of firms. Long term borrowing to finance investment and expansion becomes more expensive if interest charges are higher, so do week to week charges for an overdraft funding working capital. Consumer demand is lower for many things when mortgage payments are higher and credit is more expensive. The extent of difficulties that higher interest rates cause will vary from business to business. A cash rich firm might have less debt and some even have deposits which earn more interest at higher rates. The effect on demand for different products will depend on their income elasticities; where this is low a rise in interest rates will have little impact.

> An **interest rate** is a charge for borrowing money, normally expressed as a percentage of the amount borrowed per year. The risk of default is one influence on rates charged.
>
> The **Bank of England base rate** is used a starting point in the setting of many interest rates.

Taxation

Corporation tax takes a percentage of business profits. Corporation tax reached 45% in 1969, but is now 20% and is to drop to 18% by 2020. Obviously, firms prefer lower rates. There are allowances set against the tax for investment, for example. Some firms, particularly giant multinationals such as Amazon and Apple, use complex accounting systems to minimise their tax payments; sometimes they seem to operate close to the boundary between tax avoidance (legal) and tax evasion (illegal).

Corporation tax at least has the advantage that it is only payable when the business makes profit. Business rates, which are payable to local councils, depend on the premises firms use. A smallish shop, for example, can pay business rates of around £5,000 per year. Where retailers are struggling, this can be the difference between survival and closure. Almost all firms would like to see business rates reformed or even abolished. However, there is an opportunity cost – either services would have to be cut or other taxes would have to go up if business rate revenues fell.

Nominally, the contribution employers make to employees national insurance helps to fund benefits such as sick pay. In effect, though, this is just another form of tax. The amounts involved are relatively small compared to wage bills, but this is another expense.

In addition to paying tax, firms also have the burden of processing and collecting tax payments for the government. Most sales are liable to VAT (value added tax) at 20%. Firms are required to keep accurate records and forward the proceeds. For products with price elastic demand, a price increase due to VAT will discourage sales. It is no accident that heavier Excise Duties are charged on items with price inelastic demand – tobacco, alcoholic drink and petrol/diesel fuel.

Corporation tax is charged on business profits. This is the equivalent of income tax for firms. Business rates are taxes on premises used by firms, rather like the council tax paid on houses.

Government spending

Government spending can benefit firms in three ways. Governments buy everything from paperclips to prison operations from businesses. Since the 1980s, the number of services and activities contracted out to private sector firms has expanded considerably, so the government is a customer buying directly from more and more firms. Many firms are entirely or mainly involved in supplying the public sector, making them heavily dependent on government spending.

Some government spending is used to encourage firms to act in desirable ways. Website Gov.uk claims that 573 types of grant and support are available to firms. As one example, taking on many types of apprentice is encouraged by grants. There is also a variety of grants available for 'green' environmentally friendly action. 'Doing the right thing' can be subsidised by government. Government will also directly provide education, some training and infrastructure such as roads : things which are essential for many businesses.

Government payments to households include wages for public sector workers and benefits from child benefit to the old age pension. Households spend the majority of their income, so their receipts from government add to aggregate demand for goods and services from firms. Of course, most of the money involved is recycled from tax receipts. However, low income households spend most of their income and benefits, and some of the funding comes from taxes on richer people who tend to save more, so there is a net increase in consumer demand.

The business cycle

Over time we see fluctuations between boom and recession, as shown on Figure 16.2.

Figure 16.2. The business cycle

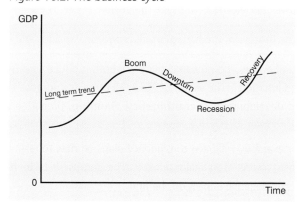

A **recession** is officially 6 months or more in which GDP (output) falls. The last recession started in 2008 and GDP took 5 years to recover to the previous level. Overall sales and revenue will fall but the impact of recession is uneven. Inferior goods, with negative income elasticities of demand, are likely to gain sales as people 'trade down'.

Organic food was steadily building its share of total UK food sales until 2008. As real incomes fell, many shoppers switched back to cheaper food from organic. British tourism might gain if people can no longer afford foreign holidays. Necessities are likely to feel relatively little impact. We need to eat and would be reluctant to give up aspects of our lifestyle which we see as necessary.

Luxuries with high income elasticities of demand are likely to suffer bigger sales reductions. Champagne sales suffer in a recession, for example. Numbers of people eating out in expensive restaurants are likely to fall, though there are likely to be more cheap takeaways eaten.

Planning to cope with a recession can reduce the impact on turnover and profits. Supermarkets, for example, can emphasise their 'value' brands and market their necessities more. Producers of luxury products might have little alternative but to cut costs to survive a difficult period, unless they can switch some of their resources to more necessary products. Even in a recession, though, there are opportunities. It is not only accountants specialising in bankruptcy who can do well despite falls in the overall level of demand.

One feature of a recession is growing unemployment. From the business perspective, this brings benefits in terms of less pressure for wage increases as people focus more on keeping their jobs. It can also make recruitment easier for firms in a position to take on labour. However, even in recession there can be skills shortages in some sub-sections of the labour market where recruitment stays difficult. Unemployment in a recession (and generally) tends to be higher for the unskilled.

Booms can bring their own problems. Pressure on resources and competition for them tends to be higher. Costs are more likely to be rising. Even whilst the economy overall is booming, there will be industries in decline and struggling to survive.

> The **business cycle** is the sequence of recession, recovery, boom and downturn which many economies go through.
>
> There is rapid GDP growth in a **boom**, often combined with high levels of employment and inflationary pressure.
>
> A **recession** involves 6 months (2 successive quarters) or more of falling GDP. This often involves a generally pessimistic business mood and falling levels of demand and employment.

Economic uncertainty

Business entails risk. Entrepreneurs know that part of their role is to manage risk. Some changes are signalled well ahead. For example, businesses know that the national minimum wage is to become 'the National Living Wage' over the next few years. They can plan for expected changes long before they arrive. Where they have no certainty, confidence is shaken and businesses become cautious. The sensible approach is to gather the best possible forecasts and to make contingency plans on how to react to sudden changes.

Official bodies such as The Bank of England and The Office of Budget Responsibility issue various forms of **economic forecast**. News media are fond of economic analysis and forecasts, though these are of variable quality. Where one of the major economic variables is particularly important to a firm, such as exchange rates to a major exporter, a business can commission or undertake forecasting of its own. Large firms often have staff of their own specialising in this type of activity.

> **Economic forecasting** is the process of predicting future economic variables and events.

Forecasting is not perfect, natural events and human activity will both produce surprises and shocks. For example, the fall in oil prices and inflation in the winter of 2014/15 came as a surprise to most people. The way to prepare for unexpected developments is **contingency planning**, preparing a course of action which could be used to respond to unexpected developments.

A sensible holiday company, for example, will have contingency plans on how to respond to a crisis (such as terrorism or economic collapse) in one of its major markets. The purpose is to be ready to respond to developments and to minimise any negative impact on the firm.

Good contingency planning starts from scenario planning, basically asking "What if... ?", combined with sensitivity analysis to measure the potential impact of different variables. Besides the internal value to a firm of knowing how to respond, the best contingency plans can also give a competitive advantage over rivals which are less well prepared.

> A **contingency plan** is a plan devised for any possible unusual development. Contingency planning is not just about major events. On a smaller scale, it's about being ready for events such as inflation and exchange rate changes, any potentially disruptive unknown.

Legislation

People are not always fair and honest. Sometimes, the temptation to cheat or cut corners in order to make a quick profit can be too strong to resist. We have a responsibility for looking after ourselves, but governments also pass laws to regulate behaviour and to protect both firms and consumers.

From the business perspective, these laws generate 'red tape' and bureaucracy which ties up time and costs money. They also restrict the behaviour of firms in ways that can be extremely frustrating. However, gains for firms include the protection they get from the consequences of other businesses behaving illegally.

Consumer protection

Various UK laws are aimed at protecting consumers. Major legislation includes:

- The **Sale of Goods Act** which says that Goods must be 'of satisfactory quality', 'fit for purpose' and 'as described by a seller'.

- The **Trades Descriptions Act** making the description of goods part of the contract between buyer and seller.

- The **Weights and Measures Act** setting out to ensure that consumers get the weight or the measure (e.g. of liquids) that are offered for sale.

- The **Consumer Protection Act** which makes sellers liable for compensation if defective products cause any damage.

- As EU citizens, UK consumers are also protected by a second layer of measures agreed by EU member countries.

- Premises that prepare or serve food are also inspected and rated under the Food Hygiene Rating Scheme, which can close unsafe premises and issues food safety ratings.

Whilst protecting consumers, such laws mean that businesses must be careful. When supermarkets sold consumers beefburgers which contained some horsemeat, it was not a sound legal defence to point out that these burgers had not been made by the supermarkets themselves and that they were unaware of the problem. The law stresses the responsibility of the seller rather than the producer. In this case the adverse publicity did more damage than a fine might have, but trading standards took a leading role in uncovering the extent of the problem.

The largest businesses have legal departments and can employ expensive lawyers to protect their interests. Small businesses are more vulnerable and a mistake could even result in closure of the business. The best approach is to take care to avoid problems by behaving legally and ethically, rather than risk problems with the law and damage to the image of the business.

Employee protection

The Employment Rights Act of 1996, other UK laws and EU provision under the Social Chapter all give employees rights. In summary, the main rights they have are to:

● receive written employment terms within a month.

● have an itemised pay slip.

● be paid at least the National Minimum Wage (The Living Wage soon).

● have holiday and maternity/paternity paid leave.

● work a maximum of 48 hours per week.

● not be discriminated against.

● be given notice of dismissal (after one month).

● receive redundancy pay or compensation for unfair dismissal (after two years).

There is a trade-off between rights which protect employees on one hand and freedom of action and costs for businesses on the other. The rights employees have make employing people, and dismissing them, more complicated and expensive than it need otherwise be. Some firms argue that treating people well is an essential part of earning their commitment and motivation, but others say that all their obligations to employees reduce flexibility in the labour market and damage both businesses and the economy.

Businesses which are determined to minimise the expense of employing people tend to rely more on zero hours contracts and 'casual' temporary employment for less than two years. This leaves people employed in this way with less rights and the firm with lower costs. Firms which do this accept the consequences of higher labour turnover and possibly less motivated employees.

> **Zero hours contracts** don't guarantee employees any hours of work. They are asked to work when wanted, e.g. when the firm is busy. There is more about this on page 71 of 'Marketing and People'.

> European Union regulations have had an impact in the UK on minimum paid holidays, working hours, equal pay, pregnancy and maternity rights and ending discrimination, for example. Opinion is divided between those who see these as important protection in a civilised society and others who resent what they see as loss of flexibility in the labour market and addition of bureaucratic red tape.

The switch from a national minimum wage (minimum £6.70 per hour for adults from October 2015, more in London) to a 'National Living Wage' is to be completed by 2020. Adults over 25 will then be paid a minimum of £9 per hour. This should lift many workers out of poverty and will save the government £billions in benefits. However, there is a clear trade-off.

Low paying industries such as retailing and care services for the elderly will face significant cost increases. Some fear that firms in these industries will have to find ways to cut their employee numbers or could even be forced out of business. A few firms might try to employ more young people as they will be relatively cheap, and offer fewer jobs to adults.

The employment of children is strictly controlled for their protection. Businesses can be fined up to £20,000 per worker for employing illegal workers. 'Knowingly' employing illegal migrants can even lead to imprisonment. There is a widespread migration crisis, with growing numbers from Africa and the Middle East seeking to move to Europe. This is an emotive issue on which some people have strong feelings.

The London sandwich making factory owned by Greencore was raided and 32 people suspected of working there illegally were arrested. Current UK government plans include seizing the wages of illegal migrants who are working and deporting them without appeal. Penalties for firms employing them are already heavy.

Environmental protection

Care for the environment covers a wide range of issues, from keeping streets and public places relatively litter free to the concern that global warming could eventually threaten the human race. Businesses have general obligations to the environment and some industries are closely monitored. The Environmental Protection Act of 1990 concentrates particularly on waste management and control of emissions into the atmosphere. Household, industrial and commercial waste is now 'controlled waste', and is regulated and managed by local authorities.

To take a simple example, Tank Industrial Maintenance Limited, based in Sheffield, was fined a total of £20,000 and ordered to pay prosecution costs of £18,000, totalling £38,000. One individual was banned from being a director for 4 years. The company, which specialised in the removal of liquid food waste, spread approximately 2,023 tonnes of liquid waste onto fields belonging to two farms. Such activity is regulated but the required 'deployment forms' and permissions had not been obtained. Cutting corners when waste built up proved very expensive.

Firms not involved in the waste industry (and households) have an obligation to dispose of waste legally. The cheap but illegal option of 'fly-tipping' (dumping and leaving waste inappropriately) can bring heavy penalties.

Activities with acidic and carbon emissions (particularly power stations) and nitrogen oxides (notably road transport) are regulated. New vehicles must meet emission standards which are slowly being tightened

The illegal option of 'fly-tipping' can bring heavy penalties.

over time. Maximum emission levels are set for existing vehicles. MOT tests check for carbon monoxide and hydrocarbon emissions, for example. For transport businesses and any other firm with multiple vehicles, compliance can bring real expense.

The UK government has made a legally binding commitment to slash greenhouse gas emissions by 60% of 1990 levels by 2030. Progress has not kept on course to meet this target. Coal and oil fired power stations are the biggest problem here. Energy producers and many other businesses must expect tighter regulation and substantial expense in order to reduce future emissions. Expansion of nuclear power is seen as one option, but this remains controversial.

Competition policy

Competition between firms can work in the interest of consumers by keeping prices down and products of acceptable quality. The Competition and Markets Authority and European competition authorities seek to combat two forms of anti-competitive behaviour. These are abuse of a dominant position by firms facing limited competition and anti-competitive agreements between firms.

50% or more market share is widely seen as a dominant position, but 25% can be taken as one indicator of a firm having some power in its market. Having a dominant position is not in itself illegal, this could just result from superior products or operations. However, a firm with a dominant position might abuse it by: excessive, predatory or discriminatory pricing; imposing unfair trading terms; or tying (bundling) where a buyer of one product is forced to buy another with it.

> There was a long running dispute between EU competition authorities and Microsoft over anti-competitive behaviour by bundling additional products such as Internet Explorer with Microsoft operating systems. This involved lengthy court actions and fines totalling the equivalent of around £1,000 million.

Few firms are caught having and abusing a dominant position, though punishments can be heavy if they are. More firms have contact with the CMA over mergers or takeovers, since there is provision for these to be blocked if they might damage competition. In 2015, for example, Poundland has offered £55 million for 99p stores. Both are 'value general merchandise retailers' basing sales on a single price point. The CMA is investigating whether this deal will result in "a substantial lessening of competition" and has the right to block the deal. In another case, scrutiny of the British Telecom (BT) £12.5bn takeover of EE mobile phone operations is likely to take the CMA several months.

Cartel behaviour is the most serious form of anti-competitive behaviour and carries the highest penalties. A 'hardcore' cartel is one which involves price-fixing, market sharing, bid rigging or limiting the supply or production of goods or services. Individuals prosecuted for a cartel may be liable to imprisonment for up to five years and/or the imposition of unlimited fines.

> A **cartel** is a group of firms which chooses not to compete but to collaborate with each other, normally with a secret deal to exploit consumers or other traders.

112 UK construction firms were accused of involvement in bid rigging, with the main allegations being against large companies involved in projects such as school and hospital building. They were thought to have agreed to put in excessively high bids, except in their agreed 'turn' to win a contract when their price was less excessive. Major UK banks were found to have colluded to fix exchange rate markets and a specialist 'Libor' interest rate to their own advantage, sometimes at the expense of their own customers. Independent schools were found to have colluded by sharing information on fee changes they planned to make.

Getting involved in cartel activity is potentially profitable but also highly dangerous. Authorities have started to 'reward' whistle blowers with more lenient treatment than other firms involved. After British Airways and Virgin Airways agreed to set identical fuel surcharges on transatlantic flights when aviation fuel became more expensive, Virgin confessed so escaped punishment. British Airways were originally fined £121.2m, though this was later reduced to £58.5m. This raises the possibility that joining a cartel and then confessing could even be used as a competitive strategy.

Health and Safety

Businesses don't set out to harm their employees or their customers, but there is a risk of negligence. The Health and Safety Executive and Local Authorities have many responsibilities arising from both UK law and EU regulation. These place many obligations on businesses. Being told that coffee may be hot, something may contain nuts, or there is another fire alarm practice can seem a waste of time to many people.

Businesses have to take reasonable steps to avoid accidents or harm; these include risk assessments and having a health and safety policy where there are more than five employees. Risk assessment means deciding what might cause harm to people and taking reasonable steps to prevent mishaps. Is there anything hazardous? What can be done to control risks? Questions such as these explain why hard hats are compulsory on construction sites, for example. Activities that carry recognised risks, such as working with chemicals, machinery or asbestos, are more heavily regulated. Firms must supply clear information, instructions and training on Health and safety to employees.

All of this can come to be seen as an excessive chore, unless and until something goes wrong. Slips and trips will happen, but firms should ensure that they are not caused by negligence or predictable hazards. More seriously, the number of fatal injuries at work was 146 in 2014/15, half the level at the turn of the century. The Health and Safety Executive can claim some credit here but there are also factors such as the decline in manufacturing activity.

> In 2010, the Deepwater Horizon drilling platform had an explosion which resulted in 11 deaths and set off a massive oil leak in the Gulf of Mexico. BP (with some subcontractors) was found guilty of negligence and misconduct. Three years later, BP's estimate of fines and compensation costs to the business was over £27bn.

BP survived by selling off assets and reducing its size. Many smaller firms which have been found guilty of Health and Safety offences after accidents and tragedies have been forced into liquidation by the resulting expense. At worst, individuals responsible for fatal accidents can be charged with manslaughter. A business which does not take Health and Safety seriously can be placing its continuing existence at risk.

Chapter 18

Competition and market size

Surf Snowdonia

After construction of a 300 metre lake (or lagoon) and equipment for artificial generation of "the longest man-made surfable waves on the planet," Surf Snowdonia opened on 1st August 2015. They claim that "our pioneering Wavegarden technology is a complete game changer because it is going to make the sport of surfing so much more accessible." Also that "we believe this is the most exciting family destination in the UK." Entrance to the site is free, but lessons and time surfing are not. There is also a dining area, bar, shop and a soft play centre.

Surf Snowdonia is at Dogarrog in North Wales, 7 miles from the main A55 North Wales arterial route. Liverpool and Manchester city centres are around 1.5 hours' drive away and the city of Chester just 50 minutes.

Questions

1. From how far are surfers likely to travel to Surf Snowdonia?

2. What is the competition for Surf Snowdonia?

3. What other businesses are likely to gain from the opening of this attraction?

The market

The competitive environment is sometimes filled with direct rivals. These include everyone who is in the same market. Within an industry, all businesses that offer the same products and services are in direct competition. For example, anyone who sells electronics is a direct competitor with other sellers of electronics. All media consulting firms are in direct competition with each other.

Defining the market is less simple than it might seem at first. An electronics retailer is in competition with supermarkets and online sellers as well as similar shops. Surf Snowdonia is unique, yet it has competition. It might draw some surfers away from Rhossili Beach on the Gower peninsula, another centre for surfing in Wales – where waves are free. However, making surfing more popular could help Rhossili too. The intention, as a 'family destination', is to draw people away from other leisure attractions. It makes more sense to consider the broader leisure market in this case.

Businesses face both direct and indirect competition. Direct rivals are often easy to identify, indirect competition from less obvious substitutes will also have an impact on any firm, so this is also worth considering. The situation is normally dynamic, with new competitors emerging and current rivals modifying their products and strategies. Only a supremely confident or a very foolish business takes no notice of its competitive environment.

Most High Streets have had a branch of WH Smith for a long time. Smith was the first chain store, with roots in the 18th century. Amongst other things, it retails newspapers, many of which are long established. This looks like a very static situation. Look deeper and the picture changes. WH Smith has been through very difficult times and has had to adapt to survive. Early in this century, it was squeezed between supermarkets developing overlapping product ranges and specialist book and music stores eating into sales. Poor performance led to a takeover bid in 2004 which later fell through. Additional product lines such as toys and confectionery have been developed and 70 Post Office branches moved into WH Smith stores in 2007/8. The competitive environment has necessitated change in the markets WH Smith operates in.

Market size: mass markets

One variable is the size of the market in which firms compete. For many manufactured products, the market is now virtually global, with only a few countries (such as North Korea) taking little part in world trade. In the first quarter of 2015, Apple sold 74.5 million iPhones and took $74.6 billion in total revenue. A market such as this typically has heavy costs of developing and launching products, then extensive economies of scale as production and sales rise. To compete 'head on' in such a market would require investment and production on a scale which only large transnational businesses can contemplate. There are also some services which are nearly global. Google has around 12 billion searches per month. Microsoft has around 90% of the computer operating system market.

> A **mass market** is a large market with high sales volumes. This often involves fairly standardised products aimed at the largest groups of consumers

The idea of a small new entrant taking on any of the global giants seems fantastic, though markets are dynamic and many giants had modest beginnings. Eventually even giant firms can shrink and die. Enron, an energy company, was the 7th largest US business with 21,000 employees and worth $90bn. Deception and false accounting led to its collapse. In the 1960s, Woolworth's was a leading UK retailer with 800 branches. Your grandparents will remember them. It was the largest UK music retailer of its time, but sold many other household and food products as well. Woolworth's failed to change with the times and its last branches closed in 2009.

Many '**oligopoly**' markets are dominated by a few large firms, and have high **concentration ratios**. Many oligopoly markets also have small firms which manage to compete. Competitive advantage helps us to understand how this can happen.

> An **oligopoly** arises where a market is dominated by a few large firms. Although market shares will be highly concentrated, there can also be smaller firms in the market. An example is energy supply in the UK where six firms dominate.
>
> **Concentration ratios** measure the combined market shares of large firms in an industry. For example, the six large suppliers of UK household energy currently have a 90% concentration ratio.

Large firms are highly likely to have advantages in price and marketing/branding, due to economies of scale and the cumulative impact of sustained heavy marketing. Few people wouldn't recognise a Coca-Cola bottle or symbol, for example. The heavy spending of many giant firms on research and development helps them stay at the forefront of technology. Just occasionally, a novel idea allows a newcomer to grow rapidly (e.g. Innocent Smoothies), but quite often the idea or the business will be bought by a giant.

Uniqueness, convenience and customer service are three ways in which small firms can differentiate themselves and create a competitive advantage. Many people like their clothes, their home décor and their bread (as examples) to be distinctive. They want to escape mass market uniformity and to feel different. A small firm can often offer individual items, perhaps made by hand, by craftsmen or by 'artisans' rather than machines.

Figure 18.1: Sources of competitive advantage

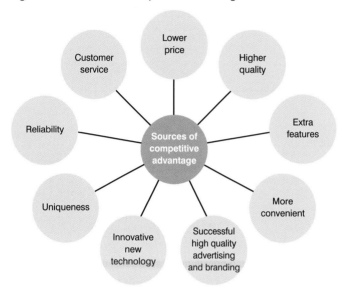

A boutique hotel is a small and stylish hotel, which are often found in urban and 'destination' areas. They make a conscious effort to stand out from large chain hotels, often with distinctive features and more personal customer service. Word of mouth and favourable reviews have helped many boutique hotels to thrive in a competitive hotel market.

Convenience stores are found in most areas, serving a localised market. Owners who live 'above the shop' can tailor opening hours to best suit their customers and develop personal relationships with regular customers. Large supermarkets have tapped into this market recently, but struggle to match the flexibility and local knowledge of independent sole traders. Just being in the right place at the right time matters. For example, the fast food market is congested but a small sandwich shop close to office blocks might be the easiest choice for workers at lunchtime.

Customer service is particularly important in personal services such as hairdressing and home maintenance, for example. There are chains which can develop branding and perhaps have cost advantages, but the trust and personal relationship which a local plumber or hairdresser can build up is difficult for a more anonymous chain to match. Closeness to clients also helps service providers to react quickly to small changes in tastes, preferences and fashions.

These possible sources of competitive advantage can also be seen in terms of the marketing mix. Small firms might not often have an advantage on price in mass markets, but they might be in the best place and they can add convenience or personalisation to their products in many cases. Another way to see the same thing might be to say that a small business can benefit from a unique selling point (USP).

The marketing mix.

Market size: niche markets

Niche markets are often too small to attract the interest of large firms. The contribution such markets might make to their revenue and balance sheet is sometimes negligible. Even small firms have to be careful. Will demand, sales volume and revenue be sufficient to recoup start-up and operating costs and make the business profitable? In a niche market there might be limited secondary market research information available, particularly information relevant to a distinctive product.

> A **niche market** is a small part of the overall market that has certain special characteristics; these may include providing a specialised or luxury product or service.

Besides the importance of information on demand, there will also be rivals in niche markets to consider. Where there is scope for a profitable small business, there is also likely to be competition. Even an original idea will not be free of competition indefinitely. If others see that a small business is profitable, they can be attracted to compete.

Competitors in niches tend to be small firms. This puts them on an equal footing unless an early entrant succeeds in establishing competitive advantage in the minds of consumers. All of the sources of competitive advantage are now potentially significant for each rival. Each firm can choose its own route to attracting and retaining sales.

Activity

Visualise a small town where a handful of estate agents sell houses for households moving out. Think of ways an agent could use each of the 9 sources of competitive advantage in Figure 18.1 (above). Which source or combination would you recommend, remembering the need for profit?

Now visualise the Chinatown area of Soho, London, where many Chinese restaurants compete. How might a restaurant seek competitive advantage?

Product and market orientation

One proactive and product orientated approach to competing entails coming up with an original idea for something not offered elsewhere. The biggest advantage of this is that there is no immediate competition to be concerned about. The big disadvantage is that the product is unproven, so the risks that consumers will not take to it or that production will prove costlier than anticipated are greater than for an established product.

> At the time of writing, Znaps are seeking crowdfunding support for their new idea. This is a small magnetic connector making it simpler and easier to link phones and other electronic devices to chargers, even in the dark, with no risk of wear or damage. Nobody can be sure of whether or not this idea will take off. If it does, sales could easily rise to the millions and the company could even perhaps find larger firms making very profitable takeover offers. If the product doesn't take off, Znaps could quickly go into liquidation with backers losing their money.

A successful trailblazing company will only have a limited start on the competition, unless it can get **patent** protection for key components. This would make direct copying of the central original innovation illegal. The value of having a start (or 'first mover advantage') consists in part of the opportunity to establish a brand name and to link the product firmly with that name. This is far easier for an established firm with a substantial marketing budget. New businesses seldom have large amounts to spend on marketing so must rely on word of mouth and seize any chance of favourable publicity. Being alive to web possibilities can help here.

A **patent** is an exclusive right granted by a government to an inventor to manufacture, use, or sell an invention for a certain number of years. The purpose of offering patents is to encourage innovation. This encourages pharmaceutical firms to take on the high costs and risks in developing new medicines, for example.

Market orientated approaches often look at ways to respond to gaps or weaknesses in a market. Market mapping and positioning can be used to identify gaps in a market where a new brand can be pitched. A related (but different) way to build market share is to identify something which current firms in a market do not appear to do well, and to focus on doing that better.

For example, if customer service is generally seen as weak a newcomer could focus on better care of customers. Insurance providers are often regarded as unresponsive and suspicious of claims. Recent adverts for both NFU Mutual and Direct line have stressed excellent customer service.

When a competitor innovates, a firm which does not respond risks getting left behind.

Exam type question

The UK Energy Market

The supply of energy to UK households is dominated by six oligopolists: British Gas, SSE, EON, EDF, Scottish Power and RWE. Ninety per cent of households buy energy from these six firms. There are smaller suppliers in the market such as First Utility and Ecotricity. These smaller firms can be cheaper; they also frequently focus on renewable energy and on good customer service.

Prices in the market fell only slowly and by limited amounts when global energy prices dropped significantly. The Competition and Markets Authority (CMA) has been investigating. Its preliminary report (July 2015) suggested that UK consumers had overpaid by around £1.2bn a year over a four year period. The six large firms seem to benefit from low price elasticity of demand. They also seem to rely on non-price competition, which is not unusual in an oligopoly market. The report also identified consumer inertia as an issue, 34% of people surveyed had not even considered switching their provider.

Questions

1. What is meant by 'oligopoly'? *(2 marks)*

2. What is meant by 'price elasticity of demand (PED)' *(2 marks)*

3. If PED is -0.5 and a supplier increases its price by 10%, what will happen to that supplier's sales and revenue? *(4 marks)*

4. Explain why large firms in an oligopoly market might prefer non-price competition. *(4 marks)*

5. Discuss two things the CMA could do to make this market more competitive. *(8 marks)*

6. Assess possible ways for smaller firms to compete in the energy market. *(10 marks)*